Detoxing
fr♥m
A Narcissist

Detoxing from

A Narcissist

12 Stages to Recovering from Narcissistic Abuse

Natalie Jambazian, LMFT

atmosphere press

To all those who have embarked on the courageous path of healing and self-discovery after enduring the pain of narcissistic abuse, this book is dedicated to you. Your strength and resilience are an inspiration. To my therapist, who has been my guiding light, your unwavering support, guidance, and empathic presence have been the cornerstone of my healing journey. Your profound impact on my life extends beyond these pages, and I am forever grateful for the transformative work we've accomplished together.

"If you are going to the trouble of choosing healthy food for your plate, shouldn't you also choose healthy people in your life?"

- Dr. Ramani Durvusula (author of *Should I Stay or Should I Go*)

"In the process of letting go, you will lose many things from the past, but you will find yourself."

- Deepak Chopra (author)

"The only person you are destined to become is the person you decide to be."

- Ralph Waldo Emerson (poet and philosopher)

CONTENTS

Introduction

You've picked this workbook for one of three reasons:

1. You recognize that you're in a relationship with a narcissist and are looking for a way out.

2. You've left a narcissistic relationship and are unsure what to do next.

3. The narcissist has discarded you, and you feel hurt, confused, and lost.

These situations all bring up big feelings—hurt, shame, grief, sadness, anxiety, anger, and depression.

Most of all, you're probably feeling defeated, betrayed, and like you have lost your sense of self.

I know how you feel because I've been there too. And, because of my personal experience, I have spent the last ten years working with survivors of narcissistic abuse in my professional life as a licensed marriage and family therapist. I have extensively researched the trauma of narcissistic abuse and its effects, facilitated groups on healing and recovering from narcissistic relationships, and helped individual clients recover from narcissistic abuse. As I worked with survivors, I realized that many of them went through similar stages. That realization is what led me to create this workbook and structure it the way I have. This workbook combines theory with my real-world experiences surviving narcissistic abuse and working with other survivors to detox and heal from their narcissistic exes.

Leaving a narcissist isn't easy, even if it isn't your choice. Narcissists love to be in charge and manipulate the people around them. They will do and say anything to keep you in their sphere of control, including making you feel like the most important person in the world, only to discard you once they no longer need you.

Narcissistic abuse can leave deep scars that go beyond feeling sad. It can manifest in different ways, including physical, emotional, and financial abuse. In some cases, a narcissist may end up in control of the survivor's emotions, leaving the survivor feeling wholly dependent on their abuser, as if they have no choice but to stay with the narcissist.

It's also possible for survivors of narcissistic abuse to develop post-traumatic stress disorder (PTSD)[1]. Several studies have found that PTSD can lead to a range of other chronic and autoimmune diseases, including inflammatory bowel disease, rheumatoid arthritis, and multiple sclerosis[2]. Further, studies have shown that experiencing long periods of stress may make your body more susceptible to developing cancer due to the long-term inflammatory response the body endures when it is under chronic stress[3].

I am not giving you this information to scare you, but rather to let you know that the physical symptoms you are feeling from being in a relationship with a narcissist are very real. Don't ignore them! And, if it's been a while since you saw a physician, now may be a good time to set up an appointment to start taking control of your physical health.

With all that being said, I want to take a moment to congratulate you for taking this first important step toward healing. You recognize that you need to recover from the hurt

----

1 (Lundberg, *The long-term effects of narcissistic abuse* 2023)

2 (Bookwalter et al., *Posttraumatic stress disorder and risk of selected autoimmune diseases among US military personnel - BMC psychiatry* 2020)

3 (Dai et al., *Chronic stress promotes cancer development* 2020)

caused by the narcissist in your life, and you acknowledge that you are worth far more than they have ever given you.

That is a big step. You should feel proud of yourself. But your work isn't over yet.

What to Expect in This Workbook

This book is for survivors of narcissistic abuse who have finally said *enough* about the patterns of abuse in their romantic relationships. It's written from a personal and clinical perspective. That's right—I know what it's like to be in a relationship with a narcissist because I was there, too.

I have experienced betrayal caused by a narcissistic partner. Over time, I have been able to heal and thrive. You would think that, as a therapist, I would have quickly caught on to a narcissist, but boy was I wrong. Narcissism wasn't taught in graduate school. My professors just skimmed through Narcissistic Personality Disorder. It was little more than a footnote in my entire graduate school career.

So, I learned about narcissists and narcissistic abuse the way you have—the hard way. After many years, I have finally discovered the formula for narcissistic abuse recovery to help survivors heal from their trauma, rewire their brains, and move forward with the rest of their lives, feeling fulfilled. After finally breaking the narcissistic abuse cycle and relearning how to love myself, I felt I had a calling to help other survivors overcome this trauma.

So, when I tell you I know what you're going through, it's because I have experienced it first-hand.

I get it. I understand it. *I've lived it.*

At first glance, I wasn't quite into my narcissistic exes (yes, there were a few). So, I avoided them until they eventually won, and I was caught under their spell.

It just took one narcissistic ex for me to awaken and finally realize their unhealthy behavioral pattern.

Even though I initially resisted their advances, the narcissist kept trying to get me into their world. Finally, after some time, I thought, "Oh, this person must really like me. They're really interested in me. I guess I should give them a chance."

Once I got hooked, it was game over for me. I was in their world. Then, one day, I suddenly woke up in a toxic relationship. It took off very fast, like a cyclone.

I started seeing the devaluation and stonewalling appear in the middle of the relationship. I started backing away, recognizing something was off and that I was unhappy.

That's when the love bombing phase set in, where I would receive subtle text messages of pictures reminding me of the relationship. That's how they sucked me back in and got me to stay. The highs were really high, and the lows were really low.

The cycle continued, and the trauma bond began.

This continued for years until one day when the narcissist found a new supply. The relationship stopped as abruptly as it had begun.

There had always been other supplies for the narcissist to feed into, but that time, it was different. That time, it was final.

I felt grief and loss. I endured the depression and all the other awful feelings that came with breaking free from this world I had been living in.

I was too ashamed to talk to my friends about what was happening. I knew it was time to see a therapist who was able to help me identify the red flags of a narcissist. Over time, through my own therapy, I healed.

So can you!

I hope this workbook brings you peace and comfort in knowing there's hope without the narcissist in your life.

It took a long time to deprogram from my narcissistic relationship. I had to undo years of self-doubt and relearn how to trust myself.

Now, I want to help you do the same thing.

It can feel scary to walk away from a relationship, even if you know it's unhealthy. But don't let fear of the unknown keep you from living the life you deserve—one full of unconditional love, respect, and happiness.

"Love is not something we give or get; it is something that we nurture and grow, a connection that can only be cultivated between two people when it exists within each one of them. We can only love others as much as we love ourselves."

- Brene Brown (author of *Daring Greatly: How the Courage to Be Vulnerable Transforms the Way We Live, Love, Parent, and Lead*)

STAGE 1:

Understanding Narcissistic Abuse

Clinically, a narcissist is defined as someone with a mental health condition who thinks they are unreasonably important compared to others. They constantly seek attention and expect to be admired at all times, even if they have not done anything to deserve adoration. They are often unable to have empathy for others. At the same time, they are often highly uncertain about their self-worth and, thus, can become quickly enraged by even a hint of criticism[4]. This is known as a narcissistic injury, which refers to the emotional turmoil narcissists feel when their egos are wounded. When they are criticized, even for minor inconveniences, narcissists will lash out in some way. It may be through aggression (either verbal or physical) or through emotional abuse, such as manipulation, walking away mid-conversation, or hurling insults at you. This exaggerated response can leave survivors feeling as if they can't offer any insight, experience any personal achievement, show any imperfections, or do anything that might cause the narcissist to feel slighted in any way. Over time, survivors can lose their identity and social support network. A narcissist will isolate a survivor until the narcissist is the only person in the survivor's life, making leaving a relationship feel challenging or even impossible.

A clinical diagnosis is not necessary for someone to exhibit

----

4. (*Narcissistic personality disorder* 2023)

narcissistic characteristics. As many as 60 million people are negatively impacted by narcissists each year[5], and an estimated five percent of the global population has Narcissistic Personality Disorder (NPD)[6]. The nature of narcissism means these individuals often don't seek therapy because they don't think they have an issue—they don't hold accountability or responsibility for their actions because they genuinely do not believe they have a problem. Instead, the survivor is the one who suffers at the hands of the narcissist by experiencing manipulation and aggression.

One of the most distinctive features of narcissism is the profound lack of empathy. Narcissists struggle to understand or care about the emotions of others. They frequently engage in manipulative tactics to achieve their goals by lying, gaslighting, and exploiting others for their own personal gain. Paradoxically, beneath their grandiose exterior, many narcissists have fragile self-esteem and can be highly sensitive to criticism or perceived slights. Narcissists need constant praise, validation, and attention from others. They require a constant stream of admiration to feel fulfilled and often become frustrated when they don't receive it.

The Five Types of Narcissists

There are five agreed-upon types of narcissists. They all share the same traits of exhibiting patterns of entitlement, grandiosity, and a general lack of empathy. But these traits can manifest in different ways for different people.

Type 1: The Overt (Grandiose) Narcissist

This is the larger-than-life narcissist, the one whom everyone seems to love and admire. They genuinely believe they are

---

5. (*60 million persons in the US negatively affected by someone else's pathology* 2010)
6. (*Narcissistic personality disorder: Traits, tests, treatment* 2020)

better than everybody and take action to make others feel the same. They have enormous self-confidence, even when it is not deserved. Because they believe they are better than everyone, including you, they believe there is nothing they can do that is wrong. They will never take blame or accountability for their actions, but will turn things around so that others are always to blame for their failings.

Type 2: The Covert (Vulnerable) Narcissist

While the overt narcissist is who many people think of when they hear the term "narcissist" (you can surely think of celebrities and public figures who fit this description), covert narcissists are much more common to encounter in the real world[7]. These narcissists do not have self-confidence and may even harbor feelings of shame and self-doubt. They believe the world is out to get them, which means they can be sad and hostile. They are deeply insecure, and these feelings often stem from early childhood experiences that left them feeling like they could never do anything right. They cannot accept blame for their actions or wrongdoings because doing so would remind them of their inadequacies. They will take credit for others' accomplishments and use it to fill the gaping hole of loneliness that lives inside them.

Type 3: The Malignant Narcissist

This is a dark form of overt narcissism in which the narcissist is colder and more calculating. They deliberately set out to watch others fail. This is a Machiavellian form of narcissism, in which the narcissist will do anything to hurt others, regardless of their relationship. A malignant narcissist is likely to cause just as many problems for themselves as for others

---

7. (Phoenix & Whitborne, *5 types of narcissists and how to identify them* 2023)

due to their extreme paranoia and their more severe aggression toward others[8].

Type 4: The Self-Righteous/Communal Narcissist

This narcissist is highly judgmental and believes everyone should follow their strict moral code. They seek validation through their work ethic and virtues and look down upon anyone who does not abide by their prescribed moral code. They can be cold and methodical as they try to invalidate those who do not live within the confines of the world they have created for themselves.

This is a sneaky narcissist to spot, as they often appear to be selfless and want to live in the service of others. They may volunteer for community organizations or speak on behalf of marginalized groups. The difference between this type of narcissist and a genuine person who wants to help their community is that a self-righteous/communal narcissist does these actions so they can gain social power and feel a greater sense of self-importance. They do not care for their community but, instead, care about giving the appearance that they are a "good person" who cares about their community[9].

Type 5: The Antagonistic Narcissist

Researchers tend to group this type of narcissist into a subcategory of overt narcissism[10]. Antagonistic narcissists are highly competitive and view everybody as their rival. They are also arrogant and prone to starting arguments. They tend to exploit others to get their way and demonstrate that they are right and everyone else is wrong. They see everything as a competition and will do anything to win.

----

8. (Telloian, *How many types of narcissism are there?* 2021)

9. (Telloian, *How many types of narcissism are there?* 2021)

10. (Heinze et al., *Validation of an implicit measure of antagonistic narcissism* 2020)

You may be able to group your narcissistic partner or ex into one or more of these narcissistic types. Knowing what type of narcissist you are dealing with can help you determine the best way to distance yourself from them and prepare you for what they might say and do as you limit your interactions with them.

Why Narcissists Make You Feel the Way You Do

Almost every survivor I've worked with questions whether they are a narcissist. If you've ever questioned whether you're a narcissist, it means you're not. Narcissists never take responsibility. It's time for you to stop the self-blame cycle!

Throughout this book, I will remind you of one critical thing—*you are not responsible for how you have been treated by a narcissist.* They are the ones with the problem and the inability to love and care for someone as special as yourself.

For those who have never experienced narcissistic abuse, it may be difficult to understand why someone would stay with a narcissist. But it's important to remember that narcissists can be incredibly charming, especially during the early stages of a romantic relationship. They will knowingly use, abuse, and discard their victim, only to bring them back into orbit again by love bombing them with gifts and appreciation. This is known as the cycle of abuse, and it's at the core of my book. The cycle is why it's so hard for survivors to leave and why many feel stuck in an emotionally, verbally, and/or physically abusive relationship.

Narcissists slowly isolate their victims from their friends and family throughout a romantic relationship. Eventually, the survivors will find themselves alone, exhausted, depressed, anxious, sometimes financially drained, and trapped by the narcissist. Those who have children with a narcissist find that leaving the relationship can be even more intimidating, particularly if the victim believes the narcissist will take full custody or become violent. Over time, victims of narcissistic abuse can become a shell of their former selves. The abuse rewires the victim's brain to the point that they don't know who they are anymore and don't believe they can leave the relationship or make it on their own.

Being a survivor of narcissistic abuse is like being addicted to gambling. Survivors, like gamblers, become addicted to dopamine rushes. They can get wrapped up in the excitement of the narcissist's charming personality, hoping to win the jackpot of affection and warmth every time they place a bet and return to the narcissist. But, more times than not, they end up feeling dejected, rejected, and disappointed.

I use the word "detox" deliberately because getting out of an abusive relationship requires the same type of mental and physical detox as coming off of any other substance. Our brains become physically rewired after we endure abuse, so getting away from it can lead to physical symptoms[11]. This biology is why so many people go back to their narcissist after leaving—they want the dopamine rush of being acknowledged and love bombed, even though, logically, they recognize it all as a façade.

Another reason leaving a narcissist is so difficult is that narcissists love to blame survivors. They twist accountability to make it seem like the survivor is responsible for the narcissist's behavior. This is done through a process known as DARVO, which stands for Deny, Attack, and Reverse Victim and Offender. It was originally coined by Jennifer Freyd, a psychology researcher and expert on interpersonal and institutional betrayal trauma and sexual violence and discrimination within institutional settings[12].

- -

11. (Bode & Kushnick, *Proximate and Ultimate Perspectives on Romantic Love* 2021)
12. (*Jennifer Joy Freyd, PhD.*)

Breaking Down DARVO

Here is a quick overview of what the DARVO process looks like. It will likely seem familiar to any survivor of narcissistic abuse who has had the tables turned on them.

Deny

When confronted about their bad behavior, a narcissist's favorite thing to do is deny, deny, deny. They will adamantly deny anything the survivor claims they have done, often making the survivor question their memory.

When this happens, the survivor might wonder whether the narcissist's actions are as horrific as they believed them to be or if they are just blowing things out of proportion. The narcissist will continue to deny any allegations and claims the survivor makes to minimize the survivor's memory and make others question who is telling the truth.

Attack

The attack phase often happens in conjunction with the denial phase. As the narcissist denies the survivor's account of an event or series of events, they will begin shifting the focus from them to the survivor. The narcissist might accuse the survivor of being mentally ill, abusing substances, or being abusive (when the narcissist is the abusive one).

The narcissist will attack the survivor's credibility, sanity, and intentions during their attack. The survivor will be left feeling bullied and worried about what will happen if they speak up about the abuse they have endured to anyone else. They may also end up feeling some sense of guilt for causing the abuse. If this has ever happened to you, it's essential to know that you are never responsible for being abused. This is just another tactic narcissists will use to keep their hands clean and keep up appearances for others and their own ego.

Reverse Victim and Offender

During this final stage of DARVO, the narcissist will twist around who is the victim and who is the offender so that the survivor seemingly becomes the offender and the narcissist seemingly becomes the victim. The narcissist will do and say anything to make it seem as if they are the one who has been wronged, even though it is the other way around.

The point of this last stage is to distract the survivor from focusing on the abuse they have endured and instead focus all their efforts on defending their reputation. So, if you have ever found yourself defending yourself after being abused rather than talking about what the narcissist has done to you, you have likely been in this final stage of DARVO.

Reclaim Your Life (and Self-Worth) in 12 Stages

There is no doubt that leaving a narcissist is difficult, thanks to the addictive nature of the relationship and the narcissistic tendency to deny everything and make survivors feel guilty for even thinking about leaving. But that doesn't mean it's impossible. With my 12-stage program, survivors can go from being addicted to their relationship to feeling free and independent.

Through the 12 stages, we will uncover how being in a narcissistic relationship has impacted how you think, feel, and act. You might be doing things now that you never dreamed you would because of your narcissistic partner or ex, who has completely changed who you are. The exercises in this book are intended to help you regain control of your narrative and life. I want you to feel empowered. You are in the driver's seat. This is your journey to recovery and healing.

As a survivor of narcissistic abuse, I know first-hand how

it feels to watch the person you believed was "the one" reveal their true colors. I have woken up to find myself alone, completely isolated from my friends and family, feeling like I had no escape. I have experienced shame and confusion from wondering how I ended up with this type of romantic partner. I know the hope that they will someday change. This is the book I wish I would have had to help me finally get the confidence and strength I needed to break free from the toxic patterns that led me into relationships with narcissists.

All the exercises in this workbook are intended to help you, as a survivor of abuse, discover and work through the previous life experiences and trauma that led you to a narcissist in the first place. My number one goal is to help you gain confidence and self-love so you can heal and never again fall for a narcissist. Some of the exercises included in the accompanying workbook include:

- A 30-day no-contact plan and calendar
- Daily, weekly, and monthly goal-setting worksheets
- Reflection on core values
- Suggested phrases to create and enforce boundaries
- Reflections on childhood trauma
- Self-care calendar with recommendations
- Journaling prompts

I know you might feel "crazy" for experiencing this abuse. You are not crazy; you have been groomed and manipulated to think, feel, and act in a certain way—one that keeps the narcissist happy without considering your needs.

I'm right here with you and will be here every step of the way.

EXERCISE:

Circle the ones that apply to you:

The narcissist shows the following signs below:	How I feel about this person:
Cold and Rigid	Hurt and confused
Lying and manipulation	Sad and lost
Cheating	Depressed
Physical abuse	Self-Doubt
Mental Abuse	Guilt
Verbal Abuse	Shame
Does not take accountability	Isolation
Rage and aggression	Anger
Silent treatment	Powerlessness
Criticizes you	Trauma
Controlling	Physical pain
Gaslighting	Anxiety
Isolation	Constant worry
Victimizes themselves	Fear and panic
Lack of boundaries	
Lack of Empathy	
Needs constant attention and admiration	
Jealousy	

What type of narcissist are you dealing with?

Give some examples of traits the narcissist has shown:

How do you currently feel?

Write down what personal boundaries you need to set with the narcissist:

What steps will you need to take to make sure your boundaries are not violated:

"I am not what happened to me, I am what I choose to become."

- Carl Jung (psychiatrist and psychoanalyst)

STAGE 2:

Realization

At some point before picking up this book, you had an "ah-ha" moment. It might have been a slow build as you finally came out of the fog that had surrounded you for the duration of your relationship. Or something specific may have happened that suddenly woke you up and made you face the reality of your relationship.

Regardless of your path, the point at which you recognize that your relationship is toxic is referred to as "realization." It's when you realize your relationship isn't right, and you must do something drastic to get yourself out of it.

Your realization happened at some point during the narcissistic abuse cycle. This is a cycle all narcissists go through in their relationships to keep survivors within reach, even if those survivors have realized that the relationship they are in is unhealthy. As you learn about each stage, you will likely recognize moments in your relationship that encapsulate each of them.

Narcissistic Abuse Cycle

Once you enter a relationship with a narcissist, you find yourself in a continuous repetitive cycle:

Love bombing -> devaluing -> discarding ->
hoovering -> repeat

As long as you feel trapped in this cycle, it's a whirlwind toxic romance that fluctuates between periods of excitement and adoration and periods of sadness, anger, and confusion. Don't get caught up in it, especially during the love bombing stage, when you might feel as though the narcissist truly loves you. Set your boundaries and distract yourself from thinking about the narcissist by focusing on improving your mental and physical health and well-being.

The narcissistic abuse cycle is incredibly manipulative, just like the narcissists themselves. Narcissists will spend the first part of a relationship uncovering a survivor's vulnerabilities. Then, the narcissist will use these vulnerabilities to threaten the survivor, making them feel as if they can't live without the narcissist.

This cycle of abuse has boundless energy. It repeats itself over and over again until one of two things happens:

Option 1: The abuser discards the survivor forever in favor of another source to feed their fragile ego.

Option 2: The survivor puts a stop to it.

You do not have much control over option 1. So, in this book, we will assume that you are working toward option 2. By taking control of the situation and your relationship, you can finally end the cycle of abuse and keep the narcissist in your life from manipulating and using you repeatedly.

Let's take a closer look at each stage of the cycle. I am sure you can think of examples from your relationship that can be defined by each stage. This will further your realization and help you see that what has happened in your relationship is not your fault but the manipulative mechanisms of your narcissistic partner or ex is the problem.

Cycle 1: Love bombing and idealization

This stage is the first in a narcissistically abusive relationship. It's how the relationship begins and circles back after the abuser has discarded the victim. Unlike healthy romantic relationships, those relationships that start with love bombing produce intimacy faster than usual, which can make you feel like you are living a whirlwind fantasy romance.

You didn't enter into a romantic relationship expecting it to be abusive or for you to feel hurt, sad, and angry more often than not. Instead, you went into it thinking you would find love and happiness. Your assumptions felt validated when the narcissist made you feel like you were the only person on Earth.

The love bombing phase is where you feel like you met your Prince (or Princess) Charming. In many ways, it feels too good to be true, but you want to believe it so badly that you overlook several red flags. Once they have gained your attention and trust, the narcissist tells you they want a commitment to ensure that they don't have to share you with anybody else. They succeed by putting you on a pedestal and making you feel you are the only person in their life. They tell you they can't live without you and make you feel important and validated. They listen when you talk and share a surprising amount of your interests.

Here's what's really going on during this part of the relationship. During the love bombing stage, the narcissist is not falling in love with you. They don't share all of your interests, and they will not keep your secrets safe. Instead, they are grooming the survivor to get into a trusted commitment with them. During this stage, they typically send gifts or show affection that makes the survivor feel special. These gifts can be physical (e.g., cards, flowers, pictures, poems, lavish vacations) or psychological (e.g., compliments, quick commitment, constant communication, grand gestures).

When you're first being love bombed, you can't help but fall for the narcissist! They are so charming that even your closest friends might fail to see through their façade. You feel like you've found your soulmate. It's as if you are the chosen one who is lucky enough to be with this person. You trust the narcissist and feel safe enough to tell them intimate details about yourself and those close to you.

You're elated as your brain chemistry is shooting a high, fueled by dopamine, serotonin, and norepinephrine that feels oh-so-good. It's almost like you're on a magical drug that makes you feel nothing but warmth and happiness.

Unfortunately, none of what you feel during a love bombing is real. You feel like you're in a fairy tale because, in many ways, you are. Soon, the spell will lift, and you'll find yourself plummeting into a nightmare.

Love bombing is a form of psychological abuse that narcissists use to suck you into the relationship quickly. It has nothing to do with you as a person. You will keep trying to return to this stage because it feels so good. Unfortunately, the only time it will return is when the narcissist hoovers you back after discarding you. Depending on your relationship, you may go through love bombing a few times, or it might cycle back more frequently.

Cycle 2: Devaluing

This stage is why leaving a narcissistic relationship is so hard.

After a love bombing and idealization stage, your brain is high on dopamine. It will start to feel physical withdrawals during the devaluation stage, causing a chemical imbalance. You become chemically addicted to this cycle as you physically crave the dopamine rush you felt during the love bombing, which is why leaving a narcissist can feel impossible.

When a narcissist starts to devalue you, you might begin to react, leading to intense mood swings. Your body goes into fight-or-flight mode, and you can get into manic phases that last for days.

Devaluing can look like many things. It can be using your personal stories and trauma that you had told them in supposed confidence against you, saying hurtful things like "You have daddy issues" or "No wonder you never had any friends."

Gaslighting is another essential part of the devaluing stage.

Gaslighting happens when someone forces you to question your reality. Abusers love using this tactic to take the blame off themselves and place it onto their victims. When done well, gaslighting can even turn your friends and family against you, making them falsely believe the lies the narcissist tells them instead of the truth as you have lived it.

Gaslighting does not only occur in intimate relationships. It also happens in every culture and society. Parents, grandparents, partners, in-laws, friends, co-workers, and bosses can gaslight you, making you feel like you are going crazy for seeing, hearing, or experiencing something distressing.

If your partner is a narcissist and you're also dealing with a narcissist elsewhere, you might begin to question the reality of everything you experience.

That's a dark place to be, and if you are in it, you should seek help from a qualified therapist who can help you process what you have been through. I want you to know that gaslighting is a prevalent abuse practice, and it is not your fault that the narcissist has used gaslighting to manipulate you. You must believe in your experiences and your ability to control the narrative.

Here are some examples of things a narcissist may say when they are gaslighting you:

- You're too sensitive.

- I never said that.

- That didn't happen.

- You sound crazy.

- I didn't mean it like that.

- You shouldn't feel that way.

- Stop playing the victim.

- You didn't remember it correctly.

- I was just joking; lighten up.

- Stop feeling sorry for yourself.

- You're not doing enough.

The thing with gaslighting is that the abuser doesn't just say these things once. They repeat it so often that you start believing them over your experiences. You start questioning your reality so much that you get to a point where you can no longer think for yourself.

Don't get sucked into thinking you're crazy, no matter what the narcissist in your life says.

Anytime you are:

- Doubting yourself,

- Having difficulty making your own judgments,

- Confused about what's good or bad, real or unreal,

- Questioning your decisions, and/or

- Changing yourself because someone told you what's right vs. wrong, what's good vs. bad

...then you are being gaslit!

When these things happen, write down the events to remind yourself of the facts. Refer to your writing to remind yourself of the truth. Don't believe anything a narcissist tells you—they are always only invested in their self-interests.

Cycle 3: Discarding

This stage can be permanent or temporary. It's common for narcissists to discard their partner because they are no longer getting the supply they need to keep the cycle of abuse going. Just as survivors become addicted to the chemical high they get from the love bombing stage, narcissists are addicted to the power they hold over survivors. So, when they feel that power wane or get bored with a particular partner, they search for another supply.

While getting the narcissist out of your life is the best thing that could happen to you, it does not feel like it at the time for a survivor experiencing cravings and withdrawals. That's why it's common for survivors of narcissistic relationships who have been discarded for another supply to question themselves, asking, "What was wrong with me?"

Here's the truth: it was NEVER about you.

The new supply the narcissist has left you for is nothing more than a tool to use for their benefit, whatever they think that is. It might be to prove to others that they aren't at fault for the relationship not working. Or it might be to validate their insecurities by parading the new supply in front of you. It could be that you have done something to indicate that the narcissist is losing their power and control over you, so they need to find a new supply from somebody who can be more easily manipulated and controlled.

Remember that image is everything to a narcissist. They will do anything to uphold what they deem to be their impeccable reputation. In today's world, social media is a prime platform to do this for them. Many narcissists have no qualms about smearing their ex-partner's name across social media to take accountability off them. If this has happened to you, know that there is nothing you could have done to prevent it. The narcissist will eventually tire of smearing your name once they find a new supply.

However, if they can't find another supply, the narcissist will come crawling back in the fourth stage, which sets the scene for the cycle to repeat.

Cycle 4: Hoovering

After discarding you, the narcissist will need a way to get you back. This is called "hoovering," referring to how they try to suck you back into the relationship after being genuinely awful to you during the devaluing stage. Objectively, it may seem like it would be impossible for a narcissist to convince someone to come back to them after they discarded the survivor and did whatever they could to tarnish the survivor's reputation online and in person. However, anyone in a long-term relationship with a narcissist knows how cunning and manipulative narcissists can be.

There are different ways of hoovering. It can range from a simple, seemingly thoughtful text explaining how they recognize that they have hurt you and promise to do better to a grandiose gesture like an expensive gift or extravagant trip. Often, hoovering occurs publicly so the narcissist can demonstrate what a great person they are to your friends, family, and whoever else the narcissist is trying to charm.

In many ways, hoovering looks like love—at least, it looks like the type of fairy tale love we have all become familiar with from TV and movies. But it's another form of manipulation that comes after a discarding phase, like gaslighting. Remember that narcissists are a type of addict—they need a steady supply to keep them going. That means they will be persistent in their showing of seeming adoration and affection.

If you are still in a relationship with a narcissist, you might have started this journey during the devaluing stage. In that case, the narcissist may decide to hoover you as you move through this workbook. This time, the difference is that you will be prepared to recognize their hoovering tactic and have a plan to keep them from succeeding. In this case, staying emotionally neutral is best, rather than falling for it or starting a fight. Instead of returning to the narcissist, go to no

The Cycle of
NARCISSISTIC ABUSE

I. IDEALIZE

A phase of immense flattery, gifts, and excessive attention to appeal to your heart, weaken your defense mechanisms, and allow you to be drawn into a whirlwind romance without even realizing it.

IV. HOOVER

The narcissist attempts to draw a victim back into an abusive relationship by any means necessary: begging, crying, guilt-tripping, projecting, blame-shifting, etc.

II. DEVALUE

This is where the victim's usefulness to the abuser has ceased. The abuser has found a new supply. Someone to replace the victim to fulfill all their needs. The victim is tormented and thrown away as if the love shared between them never existed.

III. DISCARD

This is where the victim's usefulness to the abuser has ceased. The abuser has found a new supply. Someone to replace the victim to fulfill all their needs. The victim is tormented and thrown away as if the love shared between them never existed.

contact (more on that in chapter 3) and ignore their blatant attempts to get you back into their orbit of control. Opening the gate even a little allows the narcissist to re-enter your life and continue the cycle of abuse, which is the opposite of what we want to happen. We want the narcissist out of your life so you can recover and move on with the rest of your life

Time to Break the Cycle

I hope you can see how this abusive cycle is used to manipulate you and create a trauma bond. You likely can point to moments in your relationship that you can now define as being in one of these four stages. Unfortunately, the cycle will continue as long as you allow it. Narcissists use this to keep the victim in a relationship longer than they should be. People who have never been in a narcissistic relationship fail to understand that it is the most complex and most challenging relationship to break free from. Going through the cycle again and again is pure torture for survivors.

That's why now is the time to stop the cycle of abuse. To do this, you must choose yourself. The narcissist will try to suck you back in if you have even one foot out the door. You have to be willing to set firm and stern boundaries.

Everyone has their tolerance level; at some point, you can't go on living that way and have to make a choice. The narcissist won't leave you alone. They ALWAYS come back. If they don't, it would be a dream come true because then you could grieve and would have no choice but to move on. But that's rarely the case with a narcissist.

As long as they're lonely, without a supply to feed their ego and make them feel as important as they believe they are, a narcissist will hoover you and love bomb you to convince you to stay with them. They will make you feel like this is the only relationship that has ever worked for you, so it must mean something. They will pit you against your friends and family, isolating you to the point that you might feel as if you indeed are alone in the world—except for the narcissist.

When this happens, remember that the narcissist doesn't care about you or your relationship with you; they seek only to fill a lonely void. You are not their soulmate. They may not even view you as a person with genuine thoughts and feelings. Narcissists cannot feel empathy like we do, so they genuinely do not care about how much they hurt you. Any time the narcissist acts like they are hurt by your actions, remember that they are putting on a grand display for all to see, not genuinely feeling hurt or sad that you are leaving. They only care about having you in their zone of control, and they will do and say anything to keep the power imbalance tipped in their favor.

CALL TO ACTION: Stopping the cycle

Here are some ways to gain confidence to end the cycle of abuse.

1. Write down what the narcissist says versus what you think. This will help you rationalize what's true and what is just another abusive tactic.

What the Narcissist says to you (false truth):	What you think (truth):
1.	1.
2.	2.

3.	3.
4.	4.
5.	5.

2. Study the lingo of the narcissist above. Then, use your new vocabulary to label the different tactics they use on you, i.e., love bombing, gaslighting, devaluing, discarding, and manipulating. As you get more comfortable with the language, you will recognize that YOU are not the problem!

What the narcissist says:	What tactics they are using:

"Grief can be the garden of compassion. If you keep your heart open through everything, your pain can become your greatest ally in life's search for love and wisdom."

\- Rumi (poet)

<u>STAGE 3:</u>

Grief and Loss

In many ways, the decision to leave is the worst part of getting out of a narcissistic relationship. So, if you've gotten this far, you have already done the hard part!

Once your relationship feels like it has ended, you might feel a range of emotions. You might feel disoriented and confused. You could also feel sad, angry, and frustrated.

On the flip side, you may be conflicted and start thinking about the good times in your relationship. This is called cognitive dissonance. You might wonder if you're making the right choice.

I will stop you here and tell you that feeling sad at the end of this relationship is entirely normal. However, it does not mean you must return to your narcissistic ex or continue feeling stuck. You have just been through hell and back. It will take some time to process everything that has happened throughout your relationship.

Healing from Trauma

Narcissistic relationships aren't like normal relationships. They are abusive and traumatic. So, when you finally get out of one, you must work through the trauma you experienced before moving forward with the rest of your life.

The traumatic nature of a narcissistic relationship leads to complicated grief in which you will feel a mix of the stages of grief and loss, including denial, anger, bargaining, depression, and, ultimately, acceptance.

As a narcissistic abuse survivor, you probably have signs of Post-Traumatic Stress Disorder (PTSD). These include:

- Anxiety,

- Depression,

- Inability to relax,

- Fight or flight responses, and

- Loss of self-worth.

In the fifth edition of the *Diagnostic and Statistical Manual of Mental Disorders* (DSM-5), PTSD is described as the following[13]:

A. Exposure to actual or threatened death, serious injury, or sexual violence through direct experience, witnessing the occurrence, learning of the occurrence, or experiencing repeated or extreme exposure to details of the event;

B. Intrusive symptoms of the traumatic event, such as distressing memories of the actual event;

C. Persistent avoidance of distressing memories, thoughts, or feelings about the traumatic event(s);

D. Negative alterations in cognition and mood associated with the traumatic event;

E. Marked alterations in arousal and reactivity associated with the traumatic event(s), such as irritable behavior, hypervigilance, problems with concentration, exaggerated startled response, and sleep disturbance;

---

13. CBS Publishers & Distributors, Pvt. Ltd. (2017). *Diagnostic and statistical manual of mental disorders: Dsm-5.*

F. Depersonalization, i.e., persistent or recurrent experiences of feeling detached from, and as if one were an outside observer of, one's mental process or body (e.g., feeling as though one were in a dream or feeling a sense of unreality of self); and

G. Derealization, i.e., persistent or recurrent experiences of the unreality of surroundings (e.g., the world around the individual is experienced as unreal, dreamlike, distorted, distant).

As you can imagine, most survivors experience PTSD in or during recovery from a narcissistic relationship. If you are experiencing any of the above, you are not alone, and you are NOT imagining things.

Let's get into the different emotions you may be experiencing:

Anxiety

Many survivors experience anxiety during and after a narcissistic relationship. You could also experience separation anxiety. You might feel anxious right now about being away from your narcissistic abuser. While this is a normal response, you need to work through it to forge new and healthier relationships. Remember that healing is a journey, not a destination. Everyone's healing journey is different, and there's no way to put an exact timeline on yours. In general, though, going no-contact for 30, 60, or 90 days will rewire your brain, and you will start to feel like yourself again. Rewiring your brain involves neuroplasticity, the brain's function to change and adapt throughout your life. A study from *National Geographic* states, "Scientists find that the brain promotes 'forgetting,' and that's a good thing. When new neurons grow, they overwrite old ones." It is important to rewrite your story by creating new memories, which in turn overrides the negative impact that narcissistic abuse has instilled. The article also states, "Memories are more likely to stick if they combine information and emotion." When you experience trauma, the brain associates it with sadness, which sticks like glue throughout time. By creating new memories with happy emotions, the brain will reprogram itself.

Depression

Your abuser may have constantly put you down, making you feel as if you are worthless and therefore questioning your sanity. They gaslighted you, making you feel like you were all alone in the world. Being isolated from friends and family can make you feel depressed. Common symptoms of depression include persistent sadness, loss of interest or pleasure, changes in appetite (overeating or undereating), sleep disturbances (oversleeping or undersleeping), fatigue, irritability, suicidal thoughts, and physical symptoms.

Inability to relax

One of the worst things about living with a narcissist is not knowing what they will do next. That's why so many survivors have a hard time relaxing. They are constantly on guard, waiting for the other shoe to drop. In this workbook, we'll do exercises to help you find peace so you can stop living in chaos and start making space for yourself.

Heightened startle response

Do you get triggered easily? That comes from the years you spent under the control of a narcissist. Your "fight or flight" response is in overdrive, making you extra tense and on high alert.

Loss of self-worth

You might feel like you don't matter. Your narcissist's words have become your own. Know that you *do matter*. You have value. You are *not your abuser*. Taking time to recover and heal from narcissistic abuse by doing the exercises in this workbook will help you relearn to love yourself.

Applying the Five Stages of Grief to Narcissistic Abuse

Grief is a totally normal reaction to what you are going through. Anytime we experience loss, we need time to grieve.

As you grieve, you will likely go through five different stages. They can happen in any order for any length of time. You might not even go through all of them or find yourself staying in one step for an extended period.

Stage 1: Denial

This is the stage where you know something's wrong but aren't ready (or willing) to face it. It's common for those in a narcissistically abusive relationship to stay in denial for months or even years. You know in your heart that the relationship is over. But you haven't found it within yourself to say those words out loud or create a plan to move forward.

Stage 2: Anger

It's very normal to feel anger at the injustice of a toxic relationship. You might feel angry toward your ex or yourself. Your anger could manifest in shouting and rage, or it might come out as extreme sadness. You may isolate yourself as much as possible.

Anger is a secondary emotion; there are often other emotions under the surface of anger, such as hurt, fear, sadness,

The Five
STAGES OF GRIEF

DENIAL	You keep hoping things will improve even though you know deep down the relationship's over.
ANGER	You're angry at yourself, your partner, and the world. It clouds your judgment and makes it hard to think clearly.
BARGAINING	You keep thinking, "if only I did things differently." You may negotiate with yourself to avoid ending the relationship.
DEPRESSION	You just want to be left alone with your shame and sadness. If you have thoughts of self-harm, please seek help immediately.
ACCEPTANCE	You are finally ready to move on to the next stage of life without your narcissistic partner or ex.

and frustration. It's critical to assess the root of your anger so you can work on finding ways to relieve yourself of those other emotions that hold you back.

Stage 3: Bargaining

Bargaining is a form of grief. In a narcissistic relationship, you might bargain because you don't feel ready to face your partner's wrath, manipulation, or games. You might negotiate with yourself, reflecting on the relationship and thinking, "If I said something differently, I would still be in the relationship," "What could I have done differently?" or "Should I have not said that?"

Stage 4: Depression

Feeling deep, heavy sadness at the end of your relationship is normal, and these feelings can turn into depression. You might self-isolate because you don't want to discuss your relationship with your friends or family. You may feel shame, guilt, helplessness, or hopelessness. You may overeat or undereat and oversleep or undersleep. You may experience a loss of interest or motivation, fatigue, and crying spells. You may even have thoughts of harming yourself. If you have any of these thoughts, please seek help immediately. I have included resources at the back of this workbook to help you see through the darkness.

Stage 5: Acceptance

This stage happens when you come to terms with the many losses you have suffered—the loss of a relationship, the loss of someone you thought you could trust, and the loss of yourself.

Acceptance doesn't mean things are suddenly perfect in

your world. Instead, it indicates that you are ready to move on from your relationship to the next stage in your life without your ex.

Breaking the Cycle When You Have Kids with a Narcissist

If you have children with a narcissist, you will need to take some additional steps to break free from the narcissist. In some cases, you may still need to have the narcissist involved in your life at some level, particularly if they are granted some custodial rights with your children.

But that does not mean you need to stay in a relationship with the narcissist for the sake of your kids. In fact, I would argue that getting out of a romantic relationship with a narcissist who is daily sucking the life out of you is the healthiest thing you can do to protect your kids and provide them with a happy and healthy life.

If you are going to divorce a narcissist, you will need to be prepared for battle. Narcissists live for the thrill of getting what they want at all costs and don't care who they hurt along the way. I recommend finding a good lawyer familiar with how to handle narcissists, as they will be more prepared to face whatever manipulative tactics the narcissist attempts throughout the process.

You should also be prepared for the narcissist to use your children as pawns for their own gain. Consider seeing a family therapist who can help your children get through the divorce with as little damage as possible. Don't be afraid to be firm with the narcissist when they start trying to use your children as pawns. Set boundaries, remain calm, and always look out for your children's best interests. Do not sink to their level by using your children the same way. (We will discuss setting and keeping boundaries in Stage 4.)

When the Narcissist Won't Let Go

The grief you're experiencing might feel similar to mourning the death of a loved one. But, in many ways, it's more complex than that. Instead of being permanently removed from your life, your narcissist partner or ex is probably still trying to stay connected to you.

Narcissists love to have the last word. So, after you leave the relationship, your ex might keep sucking you back to try to hurt you. They could produce any number of threats or even start love bombing you to get you to talk to them again.

Narcissists also love to be adored. So, your ex might text you a picture of you two or send a sentimental message to lure you back to them. They will make you think they realize the error of their ways and are ready to make amends and change for the better. Do not fall for this! Once hooked on a narcissist's empty promises, you will go through the cycle of narcissistic abuse all over again.

You need to be stronger than the pull of the narcissist. You need to be the one to stop the cycle. I know it's not easy, but I'm here to guide you through the grieving process so you can heal from narcissistic abuse and find your way back to yourself.

WORKSHEET: Getting Back to Base Level

It's time to acknowledge how your narcissistic partner or ex makes you feel. Then, you need to let go and refuse to let their actions control how you live your life. This exercise will help you establish a foundation from which you can start building your new life.

Acknowledgment statements:

Use the space below to fill in these acknowledgment statements. You can repeat them out loud whenever you need to let your emotions out or let go of the control your narcissistic partner or ex has over your feelings.

I want you to know when you _____,
I felt _____,
AND I choose to liberate my pain today.

I want you to know when you _____,
I felt _____,
AND I choose not to fixate on this memory.

I want you to know when you _____,
I felt _____,
AND I choose not to give your actions power over how I feel.

I want you to know when you _____,
I felt _____,
AND I choose to remain in control of how I think, act, and feel.

Here's an example of an acknowledgment statement:

I want you to know when you were texting other people
when I was trying to talk to you,
I felt sad and hurt,
AND I choose not to give your actions power over how I feel.

"Just imagine becoming the way you used to be as a young child, before you understood the meaning of any word, before opinions took over your mind. The real you is loving, joyful, and free. The real you is just like a flower, just like the wind, just like the ocean, just like the sun."

- Miguel Angel Ruiz (author of *Four Agreements*)

STAGE 4:

Releasing Yourself from Trauma Bonding

Tell me if this sounds familiar.

You recognize that you are in a narcissistically abusive relationship and know it's in your best interest to get out.

But something is pulling you back. You can't help but think back on the good times with nostalgia. There was that trip to the Bahamas, or that time he was really sweet to your best friend.

What you're experiencing is called cognitive dissonance. It is a coping mechanism survivors use after being discarded. Lyon Festinger coined the term cognitive dissonance to describe an inconsistency between beliefs and behaviors that causes an uncomfortable feeling. It is a tactic the narcissist uses to make you feel confused about your own reality. Their actions counter the words coming out of their mouth. They distort your reality of what is real and what is not. You then blame yourself and end up apologizing for doing nothing wrong. You may start justifying their actions by saying things like "he/she had an abusive parent," "maybe they were in a bad mood," "maybe I am the narcissist," or "maybe I did something wrong."

These are examples of how victims justify being manipulated and gaslit for so long. You create a false narrative that you start believing instead of the truth. There's a longing for a time when you felt protected and loved by the narcissist, and you think walking away puts you at risk of never finding happiness.

Do not doubt yourself! You were not at fault for the destruction of this relationship.

What you're experiencing isn't love. It's trauma bonding.

The term "trauma bonding" was coined by Dr. Patrick Carnes in 1997 to describe the intense physical and emotional attachment a victim feels to their abuser[14].

You feel this attachment because of the abuse cycle we discussed previously. After your abuser discards you, they love bomb you. They elevate you by putting you on a pedestal and showering you with gifts and affection before moving on to the next stage of the cycle. This is where the addiction comes in—as a survivor, you become addicted to the hope that the narcissist will give you attention and adoration. Every time you interact with them, you get the same rush as a gambler pulling the handle on the slot machine. You may risk losing, but you also think you can win a jackpot if you keep playing long enough and trying hard.

Unfortunately, like a gambling addiction, survivors of narcissistic abuse will only end up feeling empty, broke, and disappointed. You will never hit the jackpot when you return to a narcissist. The true sign of winning will only happen after you finally leave the narcissist and begin living the life you deserve.

When you start to doubt your ability and willingness to leave a narcissistically abusive relationship, it's critical to remember that you aren't nostalgic for a genuinely loving relationship—that relationship never existed. It was all a fantasy that the narcissist created for you in the hopes of getting you to give up everything for them. Instead of genuinely loving and caring for you the way you deserve, your abuser gave you the impression that they had intense feelings of affection before devaluing you and discarding you to find a new supply.

----

14. (Carnes, *CSAT Trauma Bonds Course - Healing Tree*)

See, narcissists are addicts too—they feed off the partner who will drop everything and everyone they care about for the hope of the narcissist giving them attention. Once you stop being the source of the narcissist's ego, they will leave you and find a new one.

Signs of Trauma Bonding

Humans connect on a biochemical level. For those in abusive relationships, the chemicals that make you feel stressed all the time keep you from leaving the relationship in the first place. The two neurochemicals primarily responsible for this phenomenon are dopamine and oxytocin. Dopamine is a chemical we often correlate with instant gratification. For example, a gambler gets a hit of dopamine every time they pull the slot machine handle, thanks to the anticipation that a jackpot might be waiting for them on the other side. Oxytocin is sometimes called "the love drug" because it is associated with relationship building and trust. In healthy romantic partnerships, couples release oxytocin when they hug or engage in other physical activities.

When you are in a narcissistic relationship, these chemicals can become dysregulated, meaning you feel as if you are loved and valued when, really, the opposite is true. Survivors of abuse may even do hazardous things for their health and well-being because of these chemicals, wrongly believing they are taking action for love. Despite being abused, survivors often feel rewarded because of this chemical imbalance. This makes being in a narcissistically abusive relationship so addictive—you crave dopamine and oxytocin and feel rewarded even when you are not experiencing them as you should. You may feel genuine withdrawal symptoms when you attempt to leave your abuser because these chemicals are not reacting like you are used to. You are, quite literally, addicted to your relationship. Even when you do leave, you may find yourself with cravings to be back in the toxic relationship, which is one reason why so many people stay in abusive relationships long after they realize it is not in their best interest.

It sounds counterintuitive, but it is common for survivors of narcissistic abuse to feel closer to their abuser as they become more dependent on their abuser for everything from feeling validated to having financial security and a roof over their head[15]. This is often called "Stockholm syndrome," where victims of abuse develop an attachment to their abuser. It can make a victim feel emotionally connected to the narcissist who has harmed or controlled them.

Unfortunately, many associate a "intense" bond with a positive one. You may feel like you have a strong bond with your narcissistic partner or ex because you feel so much anxiety about leaving them: "It must be because I really love him!" You may also think your narcissistic partner or ex treats you a certain way because they genuinely love you.

The opposite is true—you feel a negative strong bond that harms your mental, physical, and spiritual well-being. It's what we refer to as trauma bonding.

You have likely experienced trauma bonding, even if you didn't realize there was a term to define it.

During trauma bonding:

- The relationship feels up and down, like a roller coaster, and you just want to throw up every single time you do this.

- You're angry at them and love them at the same time.

- You become obsessed and compulsive.

- You don't think you can survive without them.

----

15. (Freeman, *The spellbinding bond to narcissists and psychopaths - neurobiology - neuroinstincts: Dr. Rhonda Freeman* 2022)

- You're waiting for your abuser to come back to the love-bombing phase.

See if you can relate to any of these signs of trauma bonding:

- Having obsessive thoughts about the narcissist who hurt you, even if they are not present in your life;

- Seeking contact with the narcissist who you know will only cause you more pain;

- Going out of your way to help the narcissist who is only destructive to you;

- Doing whatever it takes to get the narcissist to notice and praise you;

- Trusting a narcissist even though their behavioral patterns tell you they are untrustworthy;

- Explaining away a narcissist's behavior to friends and family members;

- Holding on to secrets of the abuse or exploitation a narcissist has put you through; or

- Staying in contact with a narcissist who denies any acknowledgment or responsibility for their behavior.

It's common for victims to develop a co-dependency with their abuse as part of trauma bonding. Humans are naturally wired to form bonds with those around us. It's a survival mechanism.

So, the victim becomes dependent on the narcissist. They live for the love bombing stage, convincing themselves that the narcissist "didn't really mean it" or "won't do that again." Things are OK for a while until it's time for the narcissist to devalue and discard their victim.

There is no need to feel shame or guilt for feeling dependent on your narcissist. However, right now, you need to recognize that you are not reliant on them. You are fully capable of taking ownership of your life. You owe yourself to stop the cycle and escape this abusive relationship.

Release Yourself from the Trauma Bond

This type of relationship isn't love; it's torture.

First, you need to know that getting out of the trauma bond stage is entirely possible! I can't even tell you the number of times I have heard survivors say they can't leave a toxic relationship because they believe they can't find anyone better and it's too late for them. Unfortunately, a narcissist has groomed and manipulated them to believe this narrative. They end up wasting a lot of time in a miserable relationship instead of recognizing the power they have to be happy.

If you feel the same way—like you will never find anything better than what you have right now—know it's not true. Your life starts when you let go of this toxic cycle.

Ways to break free of the trauma bond

It's not easy breaking the trauma bond because you feel addicted to this relationship. So, if you are still in a relationship with a narcissist and feel that trauma bond, don't be too hard on yourself. It can take years to learn to break free. The work you start right now will be worth it. I promise.

I hope you feel ready to finally feel liberated from the narcissist who has been holding you back. Here are things you can do to finally break free from the trauma bond and start living the life you deserve.

1. Change the narrative. Remind yourself that you don't owe the narcissist anything. You do not need

them for anything. Only YOU can take control of your life.

2. Stop trying to change the narcissist or believing that they have the potential to become the person you want them to be. It won't work because they don't want to change. They are quite content living the way they do and genuinely do not care who they hurt to get what they want.

3. Stop thinking things will get better. They won't until you break the trauma bond and leave the narcissist.

4. Stop waiting for the perfect time to leave. There will always be an excuse for sticking around, and there will never be an ideal time.

5. Trust that you are worth the pain of breaking the trauma bond and leaving the relationship. The only way to disarm the trauma bond is by staying away from the narcissist for at least a few months. The longer you are away from the narcissist, the looser those bonds become until they eventually disappear altogether.

EXERCISE: One Month of No Contact

Dr. Carnes says what those of us who have been through narcissistic abuse already know: abusive relationships are an addiction that keeps survivors sticking with their partner through the bad times because they crave the chemicals their brain releases when things are "good."

So, when I talk about detoxing from a narcissist, I mean that in a very literal sense. Leaving a narcissistic relationship requires focused attention on detoxing and rehabilitation, the same way that quitting gambling, drinking, or any other addiction does.

The only way you can move on from a narcissistic relationship is to stop having contact with the narcissist.

This might feel impossible, particularly if you still feel trauma bonded to the narcissist. And it is, of course, more challenging when you have children with a narcissist. In that case, you must limit your contact with the narcissist to only revolve around your children. Follow the no-contact rules listed below *except when you need to communicate with the narcissist for your children's benefit.*

Going no-contact with a narcissist is difficult because narcissists *love attention* and will do almost anything to get it from you. It's best to be prepared for the many ways the narcissist may try to continue seeing and hearing from you as you attempt to go no-contact with them.

Here are some things the narcissist might do when you cut off communication with them:

- Harass you with phone calls and texts,

- Visit you at home or your workplace and try to force you to talk to them,

- Gossip about you to others online and elsewhere,

- Love bomb you to try to win you back,

- Find someone else to serve as their source in the hopes that they will make you jealous enough to reach out to them, and

- Go no-contact with you to make you feel worthless.

Cutting off contact with a narcissist takes courage. It's not easy to do, knowing it will be painful. But it's essential for you to move on. Know that the misery you feel during your initial period of no contact *will end.* The narcissist will tire of chasing you and will move on to another source to give them their fix.

Please note: if you believe that your narcissistic partner

or ex may turn violent against you, your children, or anyone else, it's essential to have a backup plan. *Don't put yourself in a dangerous situation that could harm you or others.*

Rules for No Contact

There is only one rule for going no-contact with a narcissist—don't have any contact with them! But that is easier said than done. That means:

- No texting or calling; block their phone number so they can't get through. Don't answer calls from unknown numbers, as they might be the narcissist calling from another number.

- No engaging if they show up at your workplace. You can inform security officers to escort them off the premises.

- Don't answer the door if they show up at your house. If they are threatening you or your property, call the police. Get a restraining order if necessary.

- No social-media stalking; block their accounts and ensure they can't access yours.

- No contact with friends or family members who try to get you to talk to your narcissistic ex. They may not understand, and that's OK for now.

- No asking friends or family about your ex.

- No reading emails/letters they send and no sending emails/letters back.

- No listening to voicemails your ex leaves on your phone.

I know that going no-contact with the narcissist sounds challenging, and it is. You may feel physical withdrawal symptoms, like feeling anxious, getting headaches, feeling extra fatigued, or having trouble sleeping at night[16]. That's a typi-cal chemical reaction because your brain is going through the same withdrawal process as if you were trying to recover from a gambling or substance use addiction.

I recommend having a support system to turn to if you feel tempted to talk to your ex. It could be a therapist, close friend, family member, or anyone else who will listen without judgment and encourage you to stick with your no-contact rule.

Know that your narcissistic partner or ex will attempt to contact you during this time because they cannot stand the thought of you having control over them and the relation-ship. They will use various hoovering tactics to suck you back into their orbit. Some tactics will be blatant, like love bomb-ing you with gifts and compliments. Others will be less obvi-ous, like claiming they will see a therapist to get the help they need when they are just buying time. Do not believe anything the narcissist communicates with you during this time; every-thing they do is to get you back into their orbit.

Do your best as you go no-contact, but recognize that it is not uncommon for people to give up at one point or another. Most survivors of narcissistic abuse return to their narcissist at least once. In fact, researchers have found that survivors typically go back to their abusers seven times before finally leaving an abusive relationship[17]. That doesn't mean I'm encouraging you to do the same or giving you a free pass to call your ex when going no-contact starts to feel too challeng-ing; instead, it means that if you find yourself back with your narcissist, even for one night, you shouldn't let that derail all the progress you have made. It's normal to have setbacks in any type of addiction, including being addicted to a narcis-sist. The work you have put in will still be useful and help you reach your ultimate goal of detoxing from the narcissist.

- -

16. (Bode & Kushnick, *Proximate and Ultimate Perspectives on Romantic Love* 2021)

17. (Shahida Arabi, *Narcissists use trauma bonding and intermittent reinforcement to get you addicted to them: Why abuse survivors stay* 2019)

The Grey Rock Method

If you find yourself needing to engage with the narcissist for any reason, such as if you need to coordinate childcare arrangements with them, it can be helpful to employ what is known as the "grey rock method" in communication[18]. With this method, you act as cool and hard as a rock during communication. That means not giving a reaction when the narcissist says hurtful things or tries to manipulate you.

The grey rock method works because it takes away one thing narcissists live for—an emotional reaction to their hurtful words and actions. There isn't any research to support the theory that using the grey rock method will keep a narcissist at bay. However, anecdotally, many survivors find the technique useful for emotionally detaching themselves from abusive behavior. It can be an effective way to cut off the narcissist's supply and make them lose interest in you.

No-Contact Calendar

Use the calendar below to mark off each day of no contact for a full month. You can use the space to jot down how you feel or the activities you did instead of communicating with the narcissist if you'd like. This is your calendar, so use it in any way that benefits you.

By the end of the month, you will likely feel like a weight has been lifted off your shoulders. Keep practicing self-care this month, dedicating time every day to doing something that makes you happy and brings you peace.

If you backtrack on your no-contact journey, don't give up. Keep with it. Your brain will start to reset after 30 days of no contact. The longer you can go, the more clarity you will have and the easier it will be to finally leave the narcissist. Even going no-contact for five days or a week can give you the space to see what is truly going on and give you the confidence required to leave the narcissist once and for all. When

---

18. (Villines, *Grey rock method: What it is and how to use it effectively* 2023)

you hear your inner critic speaking, telling you things like "you're never going to find anyone better" or "this is a waste of time," take a breath and do something that improves your well-being. Don't listen to that inner voice because it is not you speaking; the narcissist is trying to make you believe you can't live without them.

Draw an "X" or color-in each day that you successfully go no-contact with your narcissistic partner or ex.

MONTH:

30-DAY
No Contact Calendar

Draw an "X" through each date that you successfully maintain no contact.

1	2	3	4	5
6	7	8	9	10
11	12	13	14	15
16	17	18	19	20
21	22	23	24	25
26	27	28	29	30

"To be yourself in a world that is constantly trying to make you something else is the greatest accomplishment."

- Ralph Waldo Emerson (poet and philosopher)

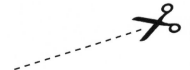

STAGE 5:

The Awakening

You now recognize that you need to get out of your relationship. However, knowing that and actually doing it are two entirely different matters. Maybe you are still on-and-off with the narcissist. You thought you went no-contact until they came back into your life and you took them back. That's OK. It happens to all survivors. You are still more conscious of and awakened to the reality that they are a narcissist. Or perhaps you have children with a narcissist and still need to interact with them from time to time. Knowing the narcissist will never change can ease some frustration and help you focus on engaging with them as productively as possible.

Whatever your situation, this chapter will help you awaken to your new reality and ground yourself in logic and facts instead of emotional manipulation. Then, you can establish boundaries and reinforce them with your narcissistic partner or ex-partner, even when you can't avoid seeing them.

Learning Better Coping Mechanisms

What's your go-to move when your narcissistic partner or ex says or does something to trigger you?

Most likely, you bend over backward, apologizing and changing (or "correcting") your behavior to whatever the narcissist wants.

Narcissists love this. They feed on your reaction and get pleasure from seeing you argue and grovel. They're thrilled when you apologize constantly. It feeds their ego and fuels their narcissism.

Your most powerful tool against your narcissist is to not react or over-explain yourself. You win when you refuse to respond to a narcissist's cold behavior and stonewalling. Ignoring a narcissist is like emotional annihilation. You need to resist the urge to argue with them. Instead, end the conversation, even if that means physically removing yourself from the same space as them.

Setting (and Enforcing) Boundaries

If you're in a relationship with a narcissist, there is a good chance that you can be classified as an empath. Empaths are people who are particularly aware of others' emotions. They are more sensitive to other people's emotions than most, which means they are more likely to prioritize others before their own.

Sound familiar? If so, you are not alone. Narcissists feed off empaths' willingness to do whatever it takes to make someone happy, even if it means putting their own needs last. Empaths are more likely than others to believe they can change the narcissist. They believe in seeing the good in people and think that they can help the narcissist become a better person with enough love, care, and affection.

You probably weren't born an empath. More likely, you had childhood experiences that led you to value and prioritize the needs of others before your own. It could be that you grew up in a physically or emotionally abusive household or are a survivor of childhood neglect.

Whatever the case, when you have spent your whole life people-pleasing to receive love and validation, the bravest thing you can do for yourself is to say "no" and set a boundary.

In some ways, the narcissist is the foil to the empath.

Both personality types tend to form due to childhood abuse. They just manifest in different ways. Narcissists can spot an empath from a mile away and use their knowledge of how empaths operate to manipulate them into doing their bidding and remaining under their control for as long as the narcissist needs a supply.

Your childhood plays a significant role in your beliefs and attitudes. The ones you learned when growing up influence who you are as an adult. You develop subconscious learned beliefs, and not all of them are healthy. To move on from a narcissistically abusive relationship, it is important to unlearn the unhealthy narratives you have repeatedly told yourself.

Some learned beliefs could be "It is not respectful to set boundaries," "You have to respect your elders even if they don't respect you," "You have to take care of other people for taking care of you," or "Having and enforcing boundaries is selfish."

When you are consistently told these things, you learn your voice doesn't matter, that you don't matter. So, you start pleasing your family and friends by being perfect in everything you do, doing things you don't want to do to gain their approval, or just going along with what they think is right or wrong, good or bad.

This created an identity for you rather than you making it for yourself. For this reason, you may feel trapped in these toxic relationships. Don't blame yourself.

Check-In: How Are Your Boundaries?

It's OK if you don't have boundaries or if they are minimal. Victims of narcissists tend to collapse their boundaries out of fear, frustration, or just plain exhaustion. Narcissists don't respond well to boundaries. They will kick, scream, and claw their way through the boundaries you set if you let them. They will even punish you by ignoring you when you try to set them, making you grovel for their attention.

However, even if it is OK to not have boundaries now, it is NOT OK to refuse to create them. You must establish firm boundaries to walk away from this relationship. That doesn't mean the narcissist will respect your boundaries. You aren't setting boundaries for them. Instead, your boundaries are set for you to take back control of your life.

I know this is challenging, especially if kids are involved in your relationship. But it is so important.

The most substantial boundary you can set for yourself is going no-contact with your narcissistic partner or ex. There are days when this will be easier than others. Remember, breaking free from a narcissist is like breaking free from any other type of addiction. You will go through a detox phase that includes withdrawals and relapses.

Of course, if you have kids with a narcissist, going no-contact is almost impossible; however, the best strategy is minimal responses and setting boundaries.

After the oxytocin disappears, you'll start living your best life. You'll be able to breathe again. You will begin to recover when you're finally out of the relationship. You'll feel peaceful as your energy returns, and you start feeling like YOU again.

Imagine ...

- No more walking on eggshells
- No more crying on the daily
- No more feeling depressed about your life
- MORE empowerment
- MORE self-care
- MORE self-love
- MORE self-worth
- Better boundaries

- Less anxiety

- More peace

It all starts by establishing boundaries and sticking to them.

You also have to remember that abuse survivors tend to have a hero complex. You may subconsciously believe you are their savior and can fix them by giving them more love. This is incredibly detrimental to you. Narcissists won't ever change. Only YOU have control over you! What you do, what you say, how you behave, your reactions versus responses—all of that is within your control, not the narcissist's.

Check the statements that sound relatable to you:

☐ I say "yes" to a request when I want to say "no."

☐ By giving more love, I will be able to change them.

☐ Maybe I am the problem.

☐ I am a people-pleaser, and it makes me happy to do things for others.

☐ I feel a responsibility to fix this relationship and fight for it.

☐ You put others' needs before yours.

☐ I have been placed into the rescuer role as a child.

☐ It is my responsibility to make my partner happy.

EXERCISE: Establishing Boundaries

You need boundaries firmly in place before you interact with a narcissist. They are not a giver; they are a soul-sucking vampire who will take every inch of your blood without hesitation.

So, take some time to determine those boundaries and how you will enforce them. That way, you will be prepared to shut down any abusive behavior or language.

1. Write down what actions are off-limits to you. This can include name-calling, cursing, yelling, or interruptions. List as many behaviors and actions as you want.

----

2. Describe how you will respond when the narcissist performs an action or behavior that crosses your boundaries. For example, you could walk away, repeat a phrase, hang up the phone, etc.

----

3. Repeat these phrases that you can use when the narcissist crosses a boundary. Say them as often as you need until they feel natural. Make any necessary adjustments—you need to believe these words and say them with conviction.

"I am confident in my choice."

"Let's agree to disagree."

"I am going to walk away now."

"I am not engaging."

"That is a personal question I am unwilling to answer."

4. Have a game plan. You will need to back up your assertions with actions. What will happen if the narcissist insists on crossing your boundaries? Think about what you will do when your boundaries are crossed now so you don't have to decide in the heat of the moment.

_____

_____

_____

Below are strategies to use when setting limits and boundaries:

"I hear you, but I am unable to do so right now."

"I feel hurt when you call me names."

"I am uncomfortable with that request."

"It's not something I can do right now."

"This is hurting my feelings, and I need to take space at the moment."

"Your perspective is different from mine."

List three boundaries you will set for yourself this week:

1. _____

2. _____

3. _____

"Love yourself first, and everything else falls into line."

- Lucille Ball (actress and comedian)

STAGE 6:

Recognizing Codependency, Enmeshment, and Attachment Styles

No matter what type of narcissist you are dealing with, there is one thing they all have in common—they are drawn to people who have a hard time setting (and sticking to) boundaries. They can find a people-pleaser out of a crowd of a thousand people.

If you are the type of person who puts everyone else's needs above your own, then you know what I'm talking about. The thing is that you were not necessarily born like that. More likely than not, something happened to you during your childhood to form you in this way through enmeshment.

How Enmeshment Can Lead You to a Narcissistic Relationship

Enmeshment refers to a lack of differentiation between yourself and others. This happens at the familial level, which is referred to as an enmeshed family. An enmeshed family is close but not in a positive way. Instead, the family is close because they have no boundaries with each other—in an enmeshed family, the lines can quickly become blurred between roles, and there is minimal tolerance for individuality or separateness.

Enmeshed families are unhealthy and fall under the category of dysfunctional. According to the family therapist who first coined the term in the 1970s, Salvador Minuchin, a typical family has three subsystems: the spouse, parental, and sibling subsystems[19]. They operate together to form a family hierarchy that should display five standard behaviors:

1. Parents nurture their children more than children nurture their parents.

2. Parents are in control of their children more than children are in control of their parents.

3. Parents are in an alliance with each other, not with their children.

4. One parent will not become an ally with their child to turn against the other parent.

5. Subsystems relate on a generational level; i.e., spouses relate more to each other than siblings and vice versa.

In an enmeshed family, at least one member deviates from one or more of these behaviors. This can lead to heightened emotions between family members, making it even more challenging for everyone to make decisions independently. There is an evident lack of boundaries between family members. While this may make it seem like the family is close (i.e., we do everything together and have the same interests and personalities), enmeshed families are highly dysfunctional. Children who come from enmeshed parents are more likely to experience lower tolerance to stress and other forms of emotional dysregulation[20].

----

19. (Liebman et al., *The use of structural family therapy in the treatment of intractable asthma* 1974)

20. (Kivisto et al., *Family enmeshment, adolescent emotional dysregulation, and the moderating role of gender* 2015)

Enmeshed parents may present a loving appearance to the outside world. However, within the family, they tend to demonstrate negative emotions, like hostility, and they are often competitive with each other and intrusive, meaning they do not care about crossing boundaries with their children. The psychological control enmeshed parents lord over their children can result in an unhealthy, codependent relationship.

Interestingly, while enmeshed families seemingly have no boundaries within the confines of the family unit, they have extreme boundaries regarding the outside world. Children in enmeshed families are often limited in how and when they interact with outsiders, leaving them to fulfill their needs within their family. They can feel shame and guilt when they do something that falls outside the familial expectations and norms, leading to a fear of abandonment that extends beyond childhood and into adulthood.

Several things can cause enmeshment in a family. In some cases, enmeshment results from a long-standing feud between parents. Parents can become enmeshed with their children as part of their conflict, forcing them to choose a side. Enmeshment can also happen when one parent is physically abusive or uses other types of severe punishment. The non-abusive parent may form an enmeshed relationship with the child.

Adult children from an enmeshed family are likely to repeat the cycle, as enmeshment is passed down from generation to generation. It's human nature to stick with what is familiar and comfortable, even if it is unhealthy. So, if you came from an enmeshed family, you did not think twice before entering an enmeshed romantic relationship.

Here are a few signs that you were or are in an enmeshed relationship:

- You are so focused on your partner's feelings that you are out of touch with your own.

- You don't have any hobbies or interests because your entire world is focused on someone else.

- You believe that you are personally responsible for the happiness and health of your partner—you feel like a failure when something bad happens to them, and they tell you it's your fault.

- You believe you can only be happy if your partner wills it—you do not know how to feel emotions independent of how your partner thinks and feels.

- You suppress your feelings because you don't want to start an argument.

- You do not feel as if you can make a decision without input from your partner.

- If you do make a decision independently, it is immediately followed by feelings of guilt and shame.

- You are physically uncomfortable spending time away from your partner.

- You have no privacy when it comes to your partner.

According to attachment theory, our attachment styles developed based on how we bonded with our primary caregivers. Just knowing these exist can help you detox from a narcissist and have a positive influence on your future relationships.

What's Your Attachment Style?

So, which one is most applicable to you? Here's a short quiz to help you figure it out. Circle the statement that applies to you. Then, tally your responses according to the key at the end of the quiz.

I worry I won't find someone else if my partner leaves me.

O   A - Yes
O   B - No
O   C - No

My partner getting too close to me makes me nervous.

O   A - No
O   B - No
O   C - Yes

I can typically argue with my partner without questioning our entire relationship.

O   A - No
O   B - Yes
O   C - No

I'm not comfortable with the level of intimacy my partner desires.

O   A - No
O   B - No
O   C - Yes

When I'm in conflict with someone, I tend to ignore reason and instead do or say things on impulse that I regret later.

O   A - Yes
O   B - No
O   C - No

I'm often called boring because I don't create a lot of drama in my relationships.

O   A - No
O   B - Yes
O   C - No

I'm worried about being unattractive.

O   A - Yes
O   B - No
O   C - No

When I'm away from my partner, I miss them, but once they return, I feel the need to escape from them.

O   A - No
O   B - No
O   C - Yes

A can comfortably express my opinions when I disagree with someone.

O   A - No
O   B - Yes
O   C - No

I don't want people to depend on me.

O   A - No
O   B - No
O   C - Yes

I might feel some short-term jealousy when a love interest checks out other people, but otherwise, I'm unfazed.

O   A - No
O   B - No
O   C - Yes

I feel depressed when I love interest checks someone else out.

O   A - Yes
O   B - No
O   C - No

I feel relieved when a love interest checks out other people because it means they're not trying to be exclusive with me.

O   A - No
O   B - No
O   C - Yes

I may be confused when someone I'm dating beings acting distant, but I'm comfortable knowing it's probably not about me.

O   A - No
O   B - Yes
O   C - No

I feel indifferent or even relieved when someone I'm dating starts acting cold and distant toward me.

O   A - No
O   B - No
O   C - Yes

I immediately worry about what I've done wrong when someone I'm dating begins acting cold and distant toward me.

O   A - Yes
O   B - No
O   C - No

If my partner broke up with me, I would do whatever it took to show them what they were missing and make them jealous.

O   A - Yes
O   B - No
O   C - No

If someone I've been dating for a few months wants to break up, I might feel hurt initially, but I would get over it pretty fast.

O   A - No

O   B - Yes

O   C - No

After getting what I want in a relationship, I'm sometimes unsure about what I want anymore.

O   A - No

O   B - No

O   C - Yes

I usually do not have a problem staying in touch with my exes because we have so much in common.

O   A - No

O   B - Yes

O   C - No

Number of As _ _ _ _ _

Number of Bs _ _ _ _ _

Number of Cs _ _ _ _ _

The column above with the highest number is the one that most likely aligns with your attachment style. Here's a quick overview of each one.

Mostly As: Anxious

An anxious attachment style comes from unstable parenting or caregiving that is out of touch with a child's needs. Parents fluctuate between being attentive and pushing children away, resulting in children never knowing what to expect from the people they depend on the most and feeling responsible for their parents' behavior. As a result, children can grow into adults who believe they are responsible for other people's feelings. It is common for survivors to have this type of attachment style.

Mostly Bs: Secure

This attachment style results when children feel secure, valued, and comforted with their caregivers. People who have a secure attachment style tend to have an easier time building strong, healthy relationships later in life. They are secure with themselves and their partners and are not prone to experiencing jealousy or trust issues.

Mostly Cs: Avoidant

Also called anxious-avoidant or dismissive-avoidant, this attachment style is insecure. It develops in children who have absent, strict, or emotionally distant caregivers. For example, if your caregivers frequently left you to fend for yourself at a young age, rejected you when you expressed an emotional need, or were reluctant to fulfill even your most basic needs, you may have developed an avoidant attachment style. Narcissists frequently have an avoidant attachment style.

Becoming Un-Enmeshed and Removing Your Attachment

There is a good chance that you are enmeshed if you are in a romantic relationship with a narcissist. And part of the enmeshment is attachment. Being attached to your narcissist is typical in a narcissistic relationship. But that doesn't mean it's healthy. Attachment takes us away from who we are and what we like, dislike, and tolerate. We end up in relationships with people who choose *for us* because we believe our opinions don't matter.

When you're attached, you are more focused on how your partner can make you happy and content than on the agency you have. You feel *they* are responsible for your happiness and get angry when they don't deliver. You feel like you don't have any power or control over your happiness, and thus, you depend on the whims of the narcissist.

The first step in awakening is recognizing that YOU and you alone are responsible for your happiness and your love for yourself.

Even though it can be deeply rooted in your life experiences that began when you were just a child, attachment is mind-based. It's all about thinking that you need someone else to be fulfilled. Eventually, attachment controls every aspect of your life—what you eat, what you wear, how you speak, who you socialize with, etc. The good news is that because it is mind-based, attachment is something that you can unlearn. You can live a life based on YOUR terms, not someone else's, and define what makes you happy instead of waiting for someone to define it for you.

What you are actually seeking is *connection*, which is heart-based. Connection is intimate, authentic, and liberating. It feels good and flows naturally. Mutual connection in partnership encourages you, uplifts you, and allows you to be JUST the way you are—no judgment, no retaliation.

"*The primary cause of unhappiness is never the situation but your thoughts about it. Be aware of the thoughts you are thinking.*"

- Eckhart Tolle (author of *The Power of Now*)

STAGE 7:

From Surviving to Healing

People don't accidentally get into relationships with narcissists. Narcissists are cold and calculating. They don't see romantic relationships as partnerships; they see them as power trips.

As an adult, you might not think about your childhood often. However, your childhood may be the key to unlocking why you fell into behavioral patterns that led to a relationship with a narcissist. That does not mean it is your fault that you ended up with a narcissist. Instead, it means that you may have learned certain behaviors and patterns that have led you to pursue a relationship with someone who will manipulate you rather than treat you with the respect you deserve.

Childhood Patterns and Learned Behavior

It is not your fault that you fell for a narcissist. In some ways, you have been training your entire life to end up in this type of relationship. Now that you understand and recognize patterns of narcissistic abuse, you can do better and take steps to ensure you never end up in this kind of relationship again.

Here are some reasons why you would attract a narcissist:

- You had a narcissistic parent.

- Your parents were uninvolved or not present.

- You experienced trauma or abuse.

- You were bullied as a young child.

- You are highly empathetic or codependent.

If you experienced any of these (or a combination of them), you might also experience physical and mental illnesses. For example, children who experience trauma during their childhood are more likely to participate in risky behavior and develop chronic conditions. The stress of living through trauma can lead to inflammation throughout the body, leading to chronic illnesses. In addition, living with chronic stress can lead to mental conditions such as depression and substance addiction and abuse.

A narcissist doesn't need to know the details about your past to recognize that you would make the perfect victim. They can see how you carry yourself and interact with the world.

If love and affection were shown to you in an abusive way growing up, you would subconsciously think that behavior is acceptable as an adult. It's familiar, so you put up with it. You accept the conditional love of a narcissist because you don't expect unconditional love. You don't believe your needs matter.

As a child, this conditional love may have come in the form of only receiving praise when you excelled in school, sports, or extracurricular activities. You would push yourself to be the best to get your parents' good attention to receive love and affection and would do anything to avoid their negative attention.

Perhaps you were the scapegoat in your family, being constantly told you were at fault, too sensitive, and overreacting. Repeatedly hearing these phrases from your parent feels like a rejection, and you start to get used to it. So, when you're in a narcissistically abusive relationship, the devaluation and discard phase of the cycle seems tolerable, even expected.

We are taught at such a young age if you behave "good," you will receive positive reinforcement. If you make a mistake, you are "bad." This sends a message to your inner child that "you aren't good enough" and you deserve the punishment.

Caregivers who are too concerned about their own problems create abandonment and inconsistency, leading you to grow up taking care of their needs instead of being taken care of. If you were raised in an abusive household, you were conditioned to be parentified, meaning you were the caregiver for your parents instead of the other way around. For this reason, you may have been attracted to toxic relationships as an adult, putting your needs aside to please your partner.

If, as a child, you didn't receive basic needs such as being listened to and acknowledged and instead were judged, compared to others, or made to feel like you weren't enough, then these behaviors become normalized to you. As an adult, you will subconsciously seek partners that follow these patterns and find yourself in the same situations you did as a child.

It's important to note *you are not responsible for what happened to you as a child.* Narcissists are cunning. Your narcissistic partner or ex recognized a need in you, one that was there due to circumstances that were outside of your control, and were taking advantage of your abusive past.

The only way to break the pattern is to understand your childhood and yourself. You can escape the cycle by consciously acknowledging what is happening and actively dismantling this narrative.

EXERCISE: Family Love

Think about your family dynamics. What type of love did you receive? Think of examples of when you were showered with love and affection. What were the circumstances that led to the outpouring of love?

Answering this question is the first step toward breaking the toxic cycle.

Childhood Dysfunctional Patterns

Early childhood experiences play a significant role in how you develop as an adult. If you had traumatic experiences as a child, then you have negative learned beliefs. Your inner child might still be present in your adult life, screaming at you, "LOVE ME," "SEE ME," "HEAR ME."

Your inner child exposes itself in times of conflict with a narcissistic partner. It asks, "Why can't you love me?" and becomes wounded, triggered, and hurt again.

To heal your adult self, you must heal your inner child. You need to protect that inner child and give it the love and attention it needs and deserves.

You need to tell your inner child, "I got you." Tell it, "You are loved," and "You are worthy."

EXERCISE: Healing the Inner Child

After thinking about how love was revealed to you as a child, you must understand how your inner child feels and why.

Now is the time to acknowledge the inner child and assure

them they are worthy of love.

Write a letter to your inner child from your adult perspective. Think about some situations that the inner child experienced that were frightening or confusing. Explain as an adult why the inner child was not at fault for what they experienced.

You can take as long as you need. You may even find that you need to write multiple letters to your inner child as you dig deeper into your past and uncover the reality of what was happening around you.

Letting Go of and Rewiring Belief Systems

The danger of romanticizing your narcissistic relationship is that you're creating hope where hope doesn't exist. No matter how much you wish things could be different, your narcissistic partner or ex will *never* give you the unconditional love you need. They are incapable of loving.

Stop lowering your standard for someone who won't give you unconditional love, support, and respect. Remember that trust and respect are earned. Don't give it so freely to those unable (and unwilling) to reciprocate.

EXERCISE: Uncovering Your Limiting Beliefs

Limiting beliefs are thought patterns we tell ourselves that prevent us from reaching our highest self. They are subconscious beliefs formed in early childhood that shape our thinking and acting.

For example, your parents may have treated you in a way that led you to believe you must respect your elders even when they hurt you. So, as an adult, you may submit to those who are rude and hurtful to you. Or maybe you were criticized for how you dressed, looked, and behaved, so you believe you must dress, look, and act in specific ways to receive love.

Some examples of limiting beliefs include:

- I'm not good enough.

- I don't deserve to be loved.

- I can't do [insert anything here]

- I won't be able to find anyone else.

- I'm not smart enough to be loved.

- It was my fault.

- I can fix them.

It can be challenging to determine your limiting beliefs because they are in your subconscious. So, you'll start by recognizing situations in which you will identify and reframe, such as staying with a narcissist even though you know they are not good for you because you think you won't find anyone better.

In this exercise, you will consider situations where you identify your beliefs. Then, you'll explain why you have that limiting belief.

Here's an example:

I can't/won't:
                        Find anyone better
Because:
                        I don't want to start all over again.

I can't/won't:

Because:

I can't/won't:

Because:

I can't/won't:

Because:

The reasons you give yourself are your limiting beliefs. Those are what we need to change.

The good news is that you can rewire your beliefs. Even though limiting beliefs are formed in childhood, you can alter them in adulthood.

The first step to doing that is recognizing your limiting beliefs. Then, you need to determine whether or not they are true. Finally, you must reframe your limiting beliefs so they no longer hold you back.

For example:

Step 1: What is the limiting belief?

"I am only loved if I give more attention to people."

Step 2: Is this true? List evidence that does or does not support the limiting belief.

No. My friends love me even though I rarely talk to them.

Step 3: Change the belief.

I am loved no matter what.

Step 1: What is the limiting belief?

Step 2: Rate your belief, from 0-10, 10=I believe it whole heartedly, 0=I don't believe it at all

----

List evidence that does NOT support this belief:

1.

2.

3.

4.

5.

6.

7.

8.

9.

10.

Step 3: Change the belief

_ _

Step 4: Now rate your new belief, 0-10, 0=I don't believe this new belief, 10=I believe this new belief whole heartedly

_ _ _ _ _ _ _ _ _ _

This process helps to develop healthier thought patterns and behaviors, fostering positive changes to your mental well-being.

Changing the narrative

Write down the story you tell yourself in your narcissistic relationship:

For example, here's my story:

My narcissistic ex would make me feel so special. He would take me traveling and to excellent restaurants. He would make it fun and make me feel I was the only one in his life. When we argued, he would tell me I wouldn't find anyone like him and make me believe I couldn't find anyone better, smarter, and more successful than him. He was hot and cold in this relationship. He then left me for another partner and started treating them better than he did me. Now, I am stuck without a partner, and my dream of starting a family feels out of reach.

Now, I'm going to change the narrative:

It's not my fault he was the way he was. There was nothing I could have done to change the circumstances. Just because he shows he is in a happier relationship doesn't mean he isn't abusive with his current partner. There are many people out there who will align with what I see in a partner. I won't give up on myself or let anyone make me feel worthless.

What's the story you tell yourself?

Now, change the narrative:

"The secret of change is to focus all of your energy not on fighting the old but on building the new."

- Socrates (philosopher)

STAGE 8:

Transformation

You're right if you feel your brain has changed since you entered a narcissistically abusive relationship.

Survivors of narcissistic abuse suffer brain trauma. Studies have found that long-term narcissistic abuse causes brain damage and autoimmune disorders[21].

The repetition of emotional injury physically shrinks the hippocampus, the part of the brain that manages learning and memory. This happens because the body emits the stress hormone cortisol, which actively attacks neurons in the hippocampus (i.e., the body's center of emotion, memory, and nervous system). Over time, cortisol shrinks the hippocampus.

You can't feel your hippocampus shrinking, but you might notice the effects. It can manifest in confusion, disorientation, dissociation, and cognitive dissonance. You might have some short-term memory loss.

At the same time as the hippocampus is shrinking, the amygdala is growing. Sometimes called the "reptilian brain," the amygdala stores emotions like guilt, envy, shame, fear, and grief. It's responsible for our fight-flight-or-freeze response and will react when it is triggered by abuse or even the memory of abuse.

When I say that you need to rewire your brain, I am being very literal. Your brain is recovering from a traumatic experience. And the longer you were in a relationship with a narcissist, the deeper the wounds are.

----

21. Saeed, K. (2017, October 20). *Long-term narcissistic abuse can cause brain damage.*

The good news is that you can rewire your brain and heal from the abuse you have survived.

Self-Care Is Not Selfish

The first thing you need to learn is that self-care is not selfish.

I spent my whole life thinking putting myself first was selfish. This way of thinking led me straight into toxic relationships. I was so concerned about other people and how they thought of me that I neglected to look within and recognize my self-worth.

This belief that taking care of yourself is selfish is a learned belief passed down from generation to generation. It keeps you from being YOU and alters your sense of self. You start internalizing what other people think and feel. This learned pattern of belief causes a lot of uncertainty, insecurity, and anxiety. It's dysfunctional and destructive to your inner self, allowing people to take advantage of your time and space.

It's so crucial for you to know that YOU MATTER. What you think MATTERS. How you feel MATTERS.

It's time for you to start finding your voice and setting boundaries. This is how you learn to love yourself.

Next, know that loving yourself isn't selfish—it's selfless!

Loving yourself starts with putting yourself first.

Are You a People-Pleaser?

Have you ever tried so hard to please and love the narcissist so much, only to be devalued and discarded later?

Victims of narcissistic abuse are often empaths who possess a hero complex, making them think they can fix or rescue the narcissist. When they realize it's not "good enough" for the narcissist, they try harder to please them more, only to be traumatized through it all.

Empaths are very forgiving, especially when narcissists present themselves as victims. An empath will feel sorry for them and take them back. This creates a never-ending carousel of hell.

The problem is that you become used to pleasing others instead of yourself. So, even after you walk away from a narcissistic relationship, you are still in the habit of doing everything for everyone around you.

I'm a former people-pleaser. I spent many years trying my hardest to gain approval and validation from others, believing that would make me feel accepted.

Most people-pleasers fear rejection and can get stuck in a relationship longer than they want. They also dislike inconveniencing anyone and feel guilty if they say no.

People-pleasers often grew up wanting to please their parents by receiving approval and acceptance. They are accustomed to conditional love and believe that they need to work hard to gain the approval of everyone in their lives.

This is toxic thinking. Only toxic people will set conditions for their love and acceptance. Not everyone in your life is toxic.

EXERCISE: Stop People-Pleasing

You won't stop being a people-pleaser overnight. Instead, you will need to put yourself first gradually.

Here are some ways to stop people-pleasing.

1. The Pause

Before immediately saying "yes" when asked to do something, pause for a moment and ask yourself if you truly are able (and willing) to do whatever you have been asked to do.

Practice: Start saying "I'll get back to you" instead of "yes" when someone asks you to do something, even if it's something you want to do. This allows you to determine if whatever is being asked of you fits into your calendar or serves your needs.

Practice: Offer alternatives if you can't (or don't want to) do what is being asked of you outright. For example, you may not want to take a half day off work to volunteer at your kid's school bake sale, but you can donate paper plates to the cause.

2. Ask for Help

I know asking for help can feel impossible, especially when you're the one who takes care of everything for everyone else. You may have the limiting belief that you don't deserve help from others or that asking for help is a sign of weakness.

The truth is that you can't do it all. Another fact is that non-toxic people want to help you! Studies show that people underestimate how willing others are to help them[22].

Practice: Practice not giving so much of yourself to friends and family, knowing that you are worth receiving their love no matter what.

Practice: Stop apologizing when you need help. You have nothing to be sorry for! Be assertive.

3. Spend Time Alone

You have had a narcissistic voice in your head for so long that you might not know who you are anymore or what you want out of life. Spending time alone will help you get to know yourself better.

Practice: Set aside time every day to be alone doing something you enjoy. If you aren't sure what you enjoy, try a few things out. For example, you could hike, join a fitness class,

---

22. Flynn, F. J., & Lake, V. K. B. (2008). If you need help, just ask: Underestimating compliance with direct requests for help.

or get into crafts. You can also meditate, journal, or read. The more time you spend alone, the more you reconnect with yourself. You will also have the freedom not to worry about anyone but yourself.

Your Self-Care Plan

After being with a narcissist, you will feel withdrawals. The times you spent with them were like a rollercoaster, adventurous and toxic. Your brain and body have learned to be in this cycle; you will have to set new routines for yourself. Learn to love your own company.

Self-care looks different for everyone. So, spend some time thinking about how you will care for yourself in the coming weeks. Use the space provided to list activities to reconnect with yourself as you heal from narcissistic abuse.

You can use this example calendar or fill in the blank calendar provided with activities that you enjoy and that bring you peace. Fill in with your own.

Sun	Mon	Tues	Weds
Spend 20 minutes outside	Go for a walk/ hike	Read a book for 10 minutes	Take a bath
Pet a dog	Tell someone what you appreciate about them	Go out with a friend	Create an upbeat playlist

Thurs	Fri	Sat
Have a dance party in your living room	Meditate for 10 minutes	Turn off your phone for 1 hour
Indulge in a face or body mask	Say hi to someone new	Purge your closet

Use the following monthly and weekly planners to line out your goals and the things you want to accomplish.

Use this daily planner to start scheduling hobbies and activities for yourself that you enjoy. This exercise is to distract you from overthinking and help you place the focus back onto yourself.

Monthly PLANNER

MONTH:

S	M	T	W	T	F	S

TOP PRIORITIES:

MONTHLY GOAL:

Weekly SELF-CARE PLANNER

SUNDAY:

MONDAY:

TUESDAY:

WEDNESDAY:

THURSDAY:

FRIDAY:

SATURDAY:

WEEKLY AFFIRMATIONS:

_____

_____

_____

_____

WEEKLY ACCOMPLISHMENTS:

_____

_____

_____

_____

Weekly SUCCESS

Answer the questions below at the end of the week. Doing this each week will remind you of your success and help you see how far you have come in your detoxing journey.

WHAT WERE MY KEY ACHIEVEMENTS THIS WEEK?

WHAT AM I PROUD OF THIS WEEK?

WHAT CHALLENGES DID I OVERCOME?

WHAT NEW SKILLS OR KNOWLEDGE DID I ACQUIRE?

HOW DID I DEMONSTRATE RESILIENCE IN THE FACE OF SETBACKS?

"If you can change your mind, you can change your life. You did not come to face reality; you came to create reality."

- Abraham Hicks (inspirational speaker)

STAGE 9:

Reclaiming Your Identity

It's normal for people coming out of a narcissistically abusive relationship to feel lost. Narcissists love to be the center of the universe; they consume your life in ways you likely don't even realize.

So, it's normal if you no longer know who you are or what you enjoy. The feeling will pass as you continue practicing self-care and getting reacquainted with yourself.

Now is also the time to start thinking about what activities you want to do and who you want to be around. This is a time to completely reinvent yourself from living in a narcissist's shadow to being the person you want to be.

Re-entering Society

Narcissists have a manipulative way of isolating you from friends, family, and acquaintances. It happens gradually and can be most noticeable during milestone events.

For example, you might recognize that you spent your last birthday celebrating with friends and family and this year alone at home, trying not to do anything to upset the narcissist. Or you might one day recognize that you have barely spent time with your friends and family, whom you once considered essential people.

That's because narcissists need full attention on them. If

they don't get it, they feel miserable and useless. They condition their victims to vanish into thin air and only spend time with them.

It happens slowly. Subconsciously, we isolate ourselves to please the narcissist. It starts by saying "no" to a girl's night so you can stay in and watch TV with the narcissist or by skipping a family event to do something that can please your narcissistic partner. Soon, years pass, and you are completely alone—except for the narcissist.

You let it get to this point because the narcissist makes you feel small and insecure when you choose anyone over them. You start to feel anxious when you're around friends, like you're doing something wrong. It gets to the point where going out with friends is no longer enjoyable because you spend the whole time worrying about what the narcissist will do when you finally get home.

Deceit's Favorite Role is Playing the Victim

Narcissists excel at playing the victim. They want to show the world they're not the problem or the reason their past relationships didn't work. That's why narcissists will continuously vilify their exes, showing others how great of a person they are by defaming their exes to others on social media or in person.

You may have experienced this already. It is incredibly hurtful, frustrating, and disappointing, especially if you have friends, family members, or acquaintances who side with the narcissist and believe you are the problem, not them.

It's awful to see the damage that narcissists continue doing to their victims after the relationship is over. As a survivor, you must ignore their behavior and refuse to pay attention or engage with it.

This is easier said than done, especially if friends or family

DATE:

Daily PLANNER

Remember to take care of yourself, including making sure you are eating enough and staying hydrated. Use this daily planner to hold yourself accountable as you prioritize your wellbeing.

TOP PRIORITIES:

_____

_____

_____

_____

TO-DO:

_____

_____

_____

_____

_____

MEALS PLANNER:

BREAKFAST:

LUNCH:

DINNER:

SNACK:

6 AM:	
7 AM:	
8 AM:	
9 AM:	
10 AM:	
11 AM:	
12 PM:	
1 PM:	
2 PM:	
3 PM:	
4 PM:	
5 PM:	
6 PM:	
7 PM:	
8 PM:	
9 PM:	
10 PM:	
11 PM:	
12 PM:	

WATER:

MOOD:
1 2 3 4 5

I'M GRATEFUL FOR:

members are still in contact with the narcissist. However, it's the only way to get the narcissist to stop.

Remember, the narcissist wants your attention. They want control over every aspect of your life, including how you feel. The cruelty will end once you stop paying attention to what they are doing and focus on yourself. You will stop being their source, and they'll leave you alone.

Of course, there will always be flying monkeys who support the narcissist and don't take the time to see what's going on. "Flying monkeys" are people who act as enablers or supporters of the manipulator. They are friends, family, co-workers who are influenced by a narcissist to do their bidding, often at the expense of others. They may spread rumors, engage in character assassination of the survivor, or even engage in direct harm to the manipulator's target. These individuals lack an independent perspective and blindly follow the narcissist's instructions. Unfortunately, it's inevitable, and you have no control over it. The best revenge is to let go and continue healing by working on yourself.

Freeing Yourself from Toxic Behaviors and People

By now, you should recognize the toxicity in your narcissistic relationship. Doing so may make you realize that others in your life are also toxic. They might champion the narcissist and believe you to be the villain.

Part of valuing yourself means not allowing toxic energy to enter your life. You don't have to give toxic people time or space. Getting rid of your ex might mean saying "goodbye" to people you thought were friends.

Don't think of removing toxic energy as eliminating things from your life. Instead, start giving yourself the time and respect you deserve. By doing this, you will naturally begin to attract people who value you.

Start valuing your time, love, respect, and worth. Toxic people will take themselves out of the picture, leaving room for people worthy of your time and attention.

EXERCISE: Expressing Your Self-Worth

We always have a choice over our thoughts, feelings, and reactions. Even when things feel like they are out of your control, they are not. If you feel that way, it just means you have been programmed to think, act, and behave in specific ways that don't fit your current needs.

I want you to spend the next week asking yourself three questions every morning:

1. Am I holding onto the past?

2. Is my past trauma stopping me from moving forward?

3. What are the beliefs I learned growing up?

Give yourself time to sit with your answers and the feelings they conjure, no matter how uncomfortable they may be. Then, tell yourself this every day:

"I feel endless blessings and happiness coming my way. Stress & hardships are fading away. I am going to experience breakthroughs. I am living in a state of gratitude, and I trust the timing of my life."

Say this out loud to yourself in the morning. Try it for a week to see how your mindset can change and affect the rest of your day.

How healthy are these 8 aspects of your life? Score yourself between 1 and 10.

DATE:

Wheel of LIFE

Review the 8 categories below and consider how you would rate each one on a scale of 1-10: with 1 = very dissatisfied and 10 = very satisfied.

Color in the segments based on your satisfaction level in each category.

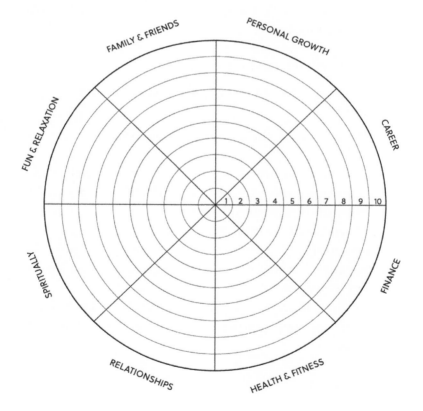

Consider your scores from the wheel of life. Describe how you will improve the areas of your life that scored less than 10.

DATE:

Wheel of LIFE

After completing the Wheel of Life, answer these questions to see how to feel about those areas in your life.

HEALTH & FITNESS

GOAL 1:
GOAL 2:

RELATIONSHIPS

GOAL 1:
GOAL 2:

SPIRITUALLY

GOAL 1:
GOAL 2:

FUN & RELAXATION

GOAL 1:
GOAL 2:

Wheel of LIFE

After completing the Wheel of Life, answer these questions to see how to feel about those areas in your life.

FAMILY & FRIENDS

GOAL 1:

GOAL 2:

PERSONAL GROWTH

GOAL 1:

GOAL 2:

CAREER

GOAL 1:

GOAL 2:

FINANCE

GOAL 1:

GOAL 2:

"Forgive yourself for not knowing what you didn't know before you learned it."

- Maya Angelou (poet)

<u>STAGE 10:</u>

Letting Go and Forgiving Yourself

Once you are awakened to the abuse you have been surviving throughout your narcissistic relationship, you might wonder how you let yourself get into that situation in the first place.

This can lead to resentment and anger toward yourself as you play the events that led you to the narcissist in the first place on a loop in your mind.

The first thing to know is that it's *not your fault* that you fell for a narcissist. However, taking responsibility for your own healing and well-being is crucial.

Narcissists groom their victims. Your narcissistic partner or ex set you up to believe every word they said, even the ones that hurt and drove you away from the people, places, and activities you used to love. They recognize that you are a kind, empathetic person ready to give your whole heart to someone. They weaponize all the things that make you a unique, caring person.

That's not on you. That's entirely on the narcissist.

Whose Voice is it Anyway?

Being on the other side of a narcissistic relationship can cause you to say hurtful things to yourself. You might think, "I'm so stupid." The question to ask is: Is this your voice or the voice of your narcissistic partner or ex?

Narcissists have a way of becoming the voice in our heads. They put us down so often that we believe what they say is true.

So, every time the voice in your head tells you something negative about yourself, stop and think about who's speaking. Chances are that it's the narcissist, not you.

That means you must retrain your inner voice to affirm the truth rather than the lie.

Changing the Narrative

It's up to you to change the narrative of how you feel about yourself after getting out of a narcissistic relationship.

Being angry won't do anything for you—I know.

Instead of constantly blaming yourself and feeling bad for how things went in your relationship, consider what you can do differently now that you are on the other side.

- How do you see the world now that you have faced this thorny challenge?

- How much stronger are you now than when you first got into that relationship?

- How can you protect yourself and your inner child so you never fall victim to a narcissist again?

I can't give you the answers to these questions. Instead, you're going to need to do some deep soul-searching work. But don't worry. I'll help you along the way.

EXERCISE: Journaling

Writing down your thoughts and feelings can release your emotions and help you figure out what's happening inside your head. Journaling externalizes your emotions versus internalizing them.

This exercise will require solitude so you can truly be alone with your thoughts. Take all the time you need to do the following activities as you work on healing yourself through forgiveness.

1. Self-forgiveness

It's common for survivors to blame themselves for ending up in a narcissistically abusive relationship. Now is the time to release your shame, guilt, and blame for yourself.

Use the following prompts to forgive yourself. Remember, YOU are not responsible for the abuse you endured. YOU are not the one at fault for what happened in your relationship.

Here are a few statements to repeat to yourself. Then, use the space provided to create your own:

I forgive myself for choosing a narcissistic partner when I didn't know any better.

I release myself from feeling ashamed for staying in this relationship as long as I did.

I absolve myself of guilt for suffering at the hands of a narcissist.

I liberate my inner child, who just wants to feel seen and heard.

I forgive myself for...

_____

I release myself from...

_____

I absolve myself of

I liberate my inner child who

----

2. Embrace the bigger picture

Now, think about the bigger picture of what was happening during your relationship. Consider what the narcissist was doing when they made you believe you weren't good enough, that you had to choose them over everything else.

Feel free to use the vocabulary discussed in this workbook, including words such as gaslighting, manipulation, limiting beliefs, codependency, love bombing, devaluing, and discarding.

----

3. Letting go

Write a letter to your former self, absolving them of their mistake in choosing the wrong person as a partner. Tell your former self that they are deserving of love and affection. Let them know you forgive them and can't wait to see who they become once they leave the relationship. Add anything else you wish someone had told you when you were still in the darkness, unaware you were falling for a narcissist.

You may burn or otherwise destroy the letter as a symbolic way of severing ties with your past self and relationship as you look forward to the future and all the great things that await you there.

"What you want exists; don't settle until you get it."

- Jay Shetty (author of *8 Rules of Love*)

STAGE 11 :

Self-Empowerment

Recovering from narcissistic abuse can take you to dark places and make you feel broken.

Repeat after me: You are NOT broken. There is nothing wrong with you. *You are not responsible for your trauma.*

Many survivors blame themselves for allowing their toxic relationships to take over their lives. They feel guilty for becoming a shadow of their former selves and allowing them to stay in an abusive relationship.

Blaming yourself for what you experienced isn't going to help. It won't turn the clock back or make the trauma you experienced magically disappear.

Instead, recognize that person as your past self. The self who endured narcissistic abuse doesn't need to be erased from history. But they also don't need to be your future. Now is the time to grieve that past self and everything they went through as you accept responsibility for your current and future healing and recovery.

Once you recognize that you are responsible for your life, choices, and transformation, you will start taking back control of your life. You'll begin to reconnect with your inner child and build a strong foundation for your future self, which doesn't include falling in love with a narcissist. Soon, you'll get to a point where you no longer become anxious when things remind you of your past.

I know this is all true because I have lived it. The inner

work that I have personally done has brought immense self-love that has led to an unshakably peaceful feeling. I have a clear vision of what I want and deserve, and I refuse to let anyone get in the way of my happiness.

You deserve happiness. But it's not going to be handed to you. You are the only one who can give yourself that gift. It's time to regain your power and remind yourself of all the reasons you deserve to be loved.

Finding Self-Empowerment Through Self-Love

Being in a narcissistic relationship can destroy your self-esteem. Narcissists love to make their victims feel like they have no control over their lives. After leaving a narcissist, you may feel anxious about making decisions, constantly playing through an eternal loop of worst-case scenarios instead of confidently making a choice.

What's happened is the narcissist has stripped away all of your autonomy. They have made you feel like you can't do anything right. No matter what you decide, it's always the wrong thing to do.

That was then. This is now.

You need to start loving yourself again to find the confidence to live on your terms—not anybody else's. The only way you can do that is by practicing acts of self-love.

Self-love doesn't mean you stop caring about other people. Instead, it means that you refuse to accept disrespect. It means setting boundaries for others to respect you physically, mentally, and psychologically. It also means appreciating yourself and your well-being enough to only surround yourself with people who value you.

EXERCISE: Getting to Know Yourself

You can't practice self-care until you spend time getting reacquainted with yourself.

This will be an ongoing process, so I recommend carrying a journal or digital notepad with you so you can jot ideas and observations down as they come to you.

Take your time answering these questions. Be as honest as possible. There are no right or wrong answers, so go with your gut. This is your space to be open with yourself! Start by considering your core values. Use the sheet provided to circle what you value most.

1. What do you like to do?

This simple question can be surprisingly tricky to answer, especially when exiting a narcissistic relationship. You may have spent the last several years doing things your ex wanted to do instead of finding activities you enjoy. As you find yourself enjoying activities, write them down.

DATE:

Your CORE VALUES

Circle the values from the list below that resonate the most with you.

INTEGRITY	OPEN-MINDEDNESS	SELF-RESPECT
RESPECT	COURAGE	SELF-WORTH
RESPONSIBILITY	OPTIMISM	SPIRITUALITY
COMPASSION	CONFIDENCE	RELIGION
ACCOUNTABILITY	JUSTICE	STABILITY
KINDNESS	SIMPLICITY	SUPPORT
UNCONDITIONAL LOVE	CURIOSITY	MEANINGFUL WORK
GROWTH	AMBITION	HUMOR
HEALING	THERAPY	FRIENDSHIPS
FAIRNESS	GRATITUDE	CONSISTENCY
AUTONOMY	PERSERVERANCE	COURTESY
ADVENTURE	FUN	MINDFULNESS
HEALTH	EMPATHY	ADAPTABILITY
CREATIVITY	TOLERANCE	DECISIVENESS
LOYALTY	BALANCE	THOUGHFULNESS
TRUST	CONTRIBUTION	LEADERSHIP
PATIENCE	HAPPINESS	

Remind yourself of these values every day. Write them down on a sticky note and put them somewhere you will see often.

2. What will you do to commit to improving these values?

----

3. Build trust in yourself

Trusting others begins with trusting yourself. So, write down some things you are committing to do for yourself. It could be exercising every day, going to bed on time, staying off social media at night, or anything else that demonstrates you are worthy of your time and love. Also, write down the self-sabotaging activities you will avoid, like binge-drinking alcohol or using other addictive substances.

_____

_____

_____

_____

_____

_____

_____

_____

_____

_____

_____

4. Feel your feelings and write them down

Survivors of narcissistic abuse tend to bury their feelings deep down inside. As you break free from a narcissist, you will start to notice yourself feeling emotions more deeply than you have been. This is a good thing, even though it sometimes feels uncomfortable or scary. Take the time to feel every emotion, even the bad ones. Observe how you feel mentally and physically during different situations. For example, how do you feel when you see a friend? Or what physical sensations do you have when you are hungry? Observe these and other feelings without judgment. Write them down.

_____

_____

_____

_____

_____

_____

_____

5. Observe your reactions

We all react instinctively to circumstances and situations that catch us off guard. Coming out of a narcissistic relationship, you may have mental and physical reactions to seeing happy couples or hearing someone mention your ex by name. Instead of rushing to cover up these initial reactions, take time to observe them. See how they evolve and write them down below.

_____

_____

_____

_____

_____

----

6. Set a goal and map out a plan to reach it

Don't shoot for the moon just yet. Instead, set a goal you believe is well within your reach. Then, map out a plan for how you will achieve it. For example, if your goal is to go to therapy once a week for a month, your plan must include finding a therapist, making weekly appointments, and attending each session. Making and achieving small goals will help you gain confidence in yourself and help you move forward with your new life. Write down small goals you want to achieve.

"Fall in love with your own solitude."

- Rupi Kaur (poet)

STAGE 12:

The New You

Self-love isn't about being selfish or refusing to make sacrifices for others. Instead, it's about NOT letting toxic people enter your life. If anyone tells you otherwise, consider it a red flag.

You allowed toxicity to enter your life before because you didn't see your value or worth. You believed toxic people when they told you to put their needs in front of your own or that you didn't have any needs. Your narcissistic partner or ex continually devalued you, making you believe that what you felt, wanted, or needed didn't matter.

For so long, you have been told how to behave, what to say, what not to say, how to dress, what's right, and what's wrong. You have been conditioned to think that your way of thinking was never right, so you let someone else decide for you. In the midst of all that, you lost your voice.

That was in the past. Now, you know better. You know you will only allow someone to treat you based on your feelings about yourself. That's why relearning who you are, what you love, and how you deserve to be treated is so important.

Saying Goodbye ... for Good

A challenging thing about breaking up with a narcissistic person is that they don't behave logically or appropriately. It's difficult to predict precisely how a narcissist will react.

One study found that people with narcissistic tendencies reacted strongly one way or another—either taking the breakup exceptionally well or extremely poorly[23]

According to the study, how a narcissist reacts will depend on the type of narcissism. Grandiose narcissists—those who are constantly seeking positive attention—are more likely to take a breakup well. They might even be the one who initiates the breakup because they have found another source to feed their need for attention.

The narcissists who tend to take breakups badly are the ones the researchers refer to as displaying signs of narcissistic rivalry. They believe everyone is a threat, and they live to demean others. Thus, breaking up with them will shatter their fragile ego, causing them to lash out in various ways.

Your narcissistic partner or ex might do the following things (and other illogical acts) during your breakup:

- Show anger towards you.

- Blame you for anything and everything.

- Spread rumors and gossip about you online and elsewhere.

- Continually try to contact you.

I'm not telling you these things to discourage you from ending it with a narcissist. Instead, I want you to be prepared and know that what you're experiencing isn't your fault. There is nothing you can do to "save" the relationship because the relationship you have been hoping for all this time never existed in the first place.

Continue practicing self-care as you move through your breakup. Surround yourself with people who lift you up, even if that means finding a new group of people to hang out with.

----

23. (Campbell et al., *Narcissistic admiration and rivalry and reactions to romantic breakup* 2021)

What Does the New You Look Like?

So, what should you expect out of the new you?

That will depend on many factors, including where you are in your relationship with a narcissist. Here are some things to expect as you move into your next life stage.

If you're still in a relationship with a narcissist

The new you won't let a narcissist make decisions on your behalf. You'll recognize when you are being gaslit and know what stage of the narcissistic abuse cycle you are in. You'll find outlets that let you be yourself and build friendships outside your relationship. Additionally, you'll stand up for yourself and refuse to engage with the narcissist when they try to manipulate you.

You may decide to exit the narcissistic relationship, or you may not. Leaving a narcissist isn't always a simple decision. Take the time you need to evaluate your life and decide what you want to do moving forward.

If you decide to leave the narcissist, you will have a support system to offer help and affirmations. You will go no-contact with the narcissist (unless necessary for co-parenting). You will not engage with or tolerate manipulation from the narcissist as you remove yourself from the relationship.

If a narcissist has discarded you

The new you will recognize that you could have done nothing to "save" the relationship because it was never a relationship to begin with. You will realize that you are better off without the narcissist. You will learn to love yourself by practicing self-care and showing yourself respect.

The new you will know that there is nothing wrong with you. You will build new relationships built on mutual trust and respect. You will not put up with anyone who attempts to gaslight or manipulate you.

If you've left a narcissist

You're free! You can go wherever you want, do whatever you want, and be whoever you want to be now that you are no longer being manipulated and controlled by a narcissist. You'll feel empowered and liberated as you face the future and all the possibilities it holds.

After you leave a narcissist, you will continue to cut off contact with them (unless you need to be in contact for co-parenting reasons). You'll find new hobbies and friends who support and respect you. You'll continue practicing self-care and become the person you have always wanted to be.

Moving On

Your story defines your growth, ambition, self-worth, and confidence. Who you were while you were in a relationship with a narcissist doesn't need to be who you are now or who you will become in the future.

Whether you are still stuck in a narcissistic relationship or recovering from one, remember you are a survivor, not a victim. Use the tools in this workbook to get reacquainted with yourself and rediscover your self-worth. Know that I'm here to support you along the way.

Getting out of a narcissistically abusive relationship is no easy task. Now that you are on the other side, it's time to figure out what you will do with your life.

The worksheets at the end of this workbook will help you define short-term and long-term goals. Use these pages to pursue the life you want and deserve.

Use this sheet to write down the goals you want to achieve in the short and long terms. Start adding goals as you get acquainted with yourself and start to envision the next stages of your life.

Start by defining your goal. Then, create a strategy of actionable steps you will take to achieve it in the goal planner section.

Relationship GOALS

Write down your top goals for your next romantic relationship.

1.

2.

3.

4.

5.

6.

7.

8.

Use this sheet to create a vision of what you want your life to look like one year from now.

Based on your goals and vision board, create a plan for yourself. Use this sheet to define your top three goals and the steps you will take to achieve them.

Vision BOARD

What is the life you envision for yourself? Use this worksheet to help you plan how you're going to get there.

I WANT TO STOP:

I WANT TO CHANGE:

I WANT TO ACHIEVE:

I WANT TO LEARN (NEW SKILL OR TOPIC):

I WANT TO CONTRIBUTE MORE TO:

Vision PLANNER

Choose 3 main goals you have for yourself. Write them down and the actions you will take to achieve them.

GOAL 1:

ACTIONS I WILL TAKE:

1. _____

2. _____

3. _____

GOAL 2:

ACTIONS I WILL TAKE:

1. _____

2. _____

3. _____

GOAL 3:

ACTIONS I WILL TAKE:

1. _____

2. _____

3. _____

Closing thoughts

Detoxing from a narcissist aims to be a beacon of hope for survivors, guiding you through the tumultuous journey of healing and self-renewal. As you embark on the path of recovery, always hold onto the belief that you deserve a life filled with unconditional love, self-compassion, and joy. The scars may linger, but they are a testament to your courage and capacity for growth and evolution. You are not alone in this journey, and you can emerge from the shadows of abuse into the radiant light of your true, authentic self. Reclaim your power, nurture your well-being, and thrive. The future holds the promise of brighter days, and your story is one of remarkable transformation, hope and triumph. As you continue your recovery process, prioritize self-care, set boundaries, and re-discover your self-worth. The transformation you seek is within your reach, and this book serves as a guiding light, illuminating the way towards a future where you are free, thriving, and living the best version of yourself.

Remember, healing is not a linear process; it's a journey not a destination. You are an evolving flower that will blossom through and through. Be patient with yourself, and allow time for the wounds to mend. Transformation is like a caterpillar's journey into a butterfly. At first, you're wrapped in a cacoon of comfort and familiarity, but as you embrace change you spin the threads of your own growth. In the darkness, you undergo a shift, shedding old patterns, identities and beliefs. Then one day, you emerge, with vibrant wings, and say to yourself "free at last". You are ready to soar to new heights, leaving behind the limitations of your past self and embracing the boundless skies of your potential. You are finally at peace, now go fly your wings.

REFERENCES

Bode, A. & Kushnick, G. (2021, March 12). *Proximate and Ultimate Perspectives on Romantic Love*. Frontiers. https://www.frontiersin. org/articles/10.3389/fpsyg.2021.573123/full

Bookwalter, D. B.; Roenfeldt, K. A.; LeardMann, C. A.; Kong, S. Y.; Riddle, M. S. & Rull, R. P. (2020, January 15). *Posttraumatic stress disorder and risk of selected autoimmune diseases among US military personnel - BMC psychiatry*. BioMed Central. https://bmcpsychiatry. biomedcentral.com/articles/10.1186/s12888-020-2432-9

Campbell, W. K.; Cheshure, A.; Kwiatkowska, M. M.; Moroz, S.; Seidman, G.; Zeigler-Hill, V.; Alexopoulos, C.; Athenstaedt, U.; Back, M. D.; Brunell, A. B.; Bushman, B. J.; Frank, S. J.; Geher, G.; Geukes, K. & Grove, J. L. (2021, October 19). *Narcissistic admiration and rivalry and reactions to romantic breakup*. Personality and Individual Differences. https://www.sciencedirect.com/science/ article/abs/pii/S0191886921007212

Carnes, P. J. (n.d.). CSAT Trauma Bonds Course - Healing Tree. https://healingtreenonprofit.org/wp-content/uploads/2016/01/ Trauma-Bonds-by-Patrick-Carnes-1.pdf

Dai, S.; Mo, Y.; Wang, Y.; Xiang, B.; Liao, Q.; Zhou, M.; Li, X.; Li, Y.; Xiong, W.; Li, G.; Guo, C. & Zeng, Z. (2020, August 19). *Chronic stress promotes cancer development*. Frontiers in oncology. https:// www.ncbi.nlm.nih.gov/pmc/articles/PMC7466429/

Flynn, F. & Lake, V. K. B. (2008). *If you need help, just ask: Underestimating compliance with direct requests for help*. Journal of personality and social psychology. https://pubmed.ncbi.nlm.nih.gov/18605856/

Freeman, R. (2022, March 14). *The spellbinding bond to narcissists and psychopaths - neurobiology - neuroinstincts: Dr. Rhonda Freeman*. Neuroinstincts. https://neuroinstincts.com/spellbinding-bond-narcissists-psychopaths-neurobiology/

Heinze, P. E.; Fatfouta, R. & Schroder-Abe, M. (2020, July 15). *Validation of an implicit measure of antagonistic narcissism*. Journal of

Research in Personality. https://www.sciencedirect.com/science/article/abs/pii/S0092656620300817

Jennifer Joy Freyd, Ph.D. Jennifer Joy Freyd, Ph.D. (n.d.). https://www.jjfreyd.com/

Jhanjee, S. (2014, April). *Evidence-based psychosocial interventions in substance use.* Indian journal of psychological medicine. https://www.ncbi.nlm.nih.gov/pmc/articles/PMC4031575/

Kivisto, K. L.; Welsh, D. P.; Darling, N. & Culpepper, C. L. (2015, August 29). *Family Enmeshment, adolescent emotional dysregulation, and the moderating role of gender.* Journal of family psychology: JFP: journal of the Division of Family Psychology of the American Psychological Association (Division 43). https://pubmed.ncbi.nlm.nih.gov/26374939/

Liebman, R.; Minuchin, S. & Baker, L. (1974). The use of structural family therapy in the treatment of intractable asthma. The American journal of psychiatry. https://pubmed.ncbi.nlm.nih.gov/4819046/

Lundberg, A. (2023, August 21). *The long-term effects of narcissistic abuse.* Charlie Health. https://www.charliehealth.com/post/the-long-term-effects-of-narcissistic-abuse

Phoenix, K. (2023, May 25). *5 types of narcissists and how to identify them.* Good Housekeeping. https://www.goodhousekeeping.com/life/relationships/a43966226/types-of-narcissism/

Publishers, C. (n.d.). *Diagnostic and statistical manual of mental disorders (DSM–5).* Default Store View. https://www.cbspd.co.in/dsm-5-diagnostic-and-statistical-manual-of-mental-disorders-5ed-spl-edition-pb-2017

Saeed, K. (2017, October 20). *Long-term narcissistic abuse can cause brain damage.* Psych Central. https://psychcentral.com/blog/liberation/2017/10/long-term-narcissistic-abuse-can-cause-brain-damage#1

Shahida Arabi, M. (2019, March 31). *Narcissists use trauma bonding and intermittent reinforcement to get you addicted to them: Why abuse survivors stay.* Psych Central. https://psychcentral.com/blog/

recovering-narcissist/2019/03/narcissists-use-trauma-bonding-and-intermittent-reinforcement-to-get-you-addicted-to-them-why-abuse-survivors-stay

Telloian, C. (2021, September 15). *How many types of narcissism are there?*. Psych Central. https://psychcentral.com/health/types-of-narcissism

Villines, Z. (2023, January 10). *Grey rock method: What it is and how to use it effectively.* Medical News Today. https://www.medicalnews today.com/articles/grey-rock

If you need to talk to someone immediately about suicide or domestic violence, contact the National Domestic Violence Hotline at 1-800-799-7233 or dial 988.

ACKNOWLEDGMENTS

Writing this book has been a journey of self-discovery, healing, growth, awareness, and empowerment. I am deeply grateful for the individuals who have supported me along the way.

To my friends and family, your unwavering love and support have been a source of strength. Your encouragement and listening ears have helped me share my voice and my story with the world. Thank you for your encouragement in creating this book and truly believing in my abilities. Thank you for being there for me through the countless tears, anxiety, and helplessness that I experienced as I was detoxing and recovering myself. Thank you for not giving up on me.

To my clients, thank you for allowing me to be part of your healing experience. Your courage and resilience inspire me every day. It is an honor to witness your transformations and learn your stories. I would like to extend my gratitude to countless survivors who have experienced this type of abuse. Your bravery has shed light on the path to recovery and has shown me that I, too, am not alone on this journey.

Lastly, to all those who have endured narcissistic abuse and are continuing their healing journey, remember that you are stronger than you know. May this book serve as a beacon of hope and a roadmap toward reclaiming your life.

ABOUT ATMOSPHERE PRESS

Founded in 2015, Atmosphere Press was built on the principles of Honesty, Transparency, Professionalism, Kindness, and Making Your Book Awesome. As an ethical and author-friendly hybrid press, we stay true to that founding mission today.

If you're a reader, enter our giveaway for a free book here:

SCAN TO ENTER
BOOK GIVEAWAY

If you're a writer, submit your manuscript for consideration here:

SCAN TO SUBMIT
MANUSCRIPT

And always feel free to visit Atmosphere Press and our authors online at atmospherepress.com. See you there soon!

ABOUT THE AUTHOR

Natalie is a licensed marriage and family therapist in private practice in Sherman Oaks, California. Natalie is a passionate advocate for healing and empowerment after narcissistic abuse. Drawing from personal and professional experience, Natalie has dedicated her career to helping survivors navigate the challenging journey to recovery and detox.

With a background in psychology, Natalie brings a unique blend of empathy and a myriad of knowledge to her passion. She understands the intricacies of narcissistic abuse and the profound impact it can have on every aspect of one's life. Natalie is an active supporter of survivor communities, both online and offline. She believes in the power of sharing stories and creating a non-judgmental and safe space for survivors to connect, heal, and thrive.

When she is not writing or working with clients, she enjoys hiking, spending time with friends and family, trying out new restaurants, traveling, reading, bike riding, and exercising.

Detoxing from a Narcissist is Natalie's first book, born from her passion for guiding survivors toward a path of recovery and resilience. She hopes this book will serve as a source of comfort and validation for all those who have faced narcissistic abuse.

Connect with her on social media, where she continues to share insights, stories, and resources on healing and growth:

https://www.tiktok.com/discover/natalie-jambazian?is_from_webapp=1&sender_device=pc

https://www.shermanoakstherapy.com/

https://www.instagram.com/selflove__society/?hl=en

9 798891 322158